I0081629

Blindsided: Your One Week Guide Toward Finding it after you've Lost it

By O. Michele Giacomini

© 2019 Dragonfly Ranch Consulting

© 2019 Dragonfly Ranch Consulting

WHO WANTS A FREEBIE???

Learn my Top Favorite 5
Tips for Success

Go to this link here today:

http://bit.ly/5SuccessTips

© 2019 Dragonfly Ranch Consulting

Copyright © 2019 O. Michele Giacomini
All rights reserved.
ISBN: 0-578-48985-8
ISBN-13:978-0-578-48985-8
Dragonfly Ranch Publishing

© 2019 Dragonfly Ranch Consulting

DEDICATION

This book is dedicated to my rock, Dave Giacomini, and
my amazing sons, Eric & Ryan Giacomini. Without you,
none of this matters. You three inspire me to be the best
me possible, each and every day.
To learn, to grow, to be open to life's new adventures.
Always.

I would also like to acknowledge some dear friends who
were either supports or inspirations for writing this book,
so that we can take the crappy lemons that life sometimes
gives us, and make our own damn lemonade and share it
with others.
Cheers to some of the best lemonade makers I know:
Sandy, Susan, Becky, Deanna, Chris, Steve,
Scott and Matt.
Let our knowledge help lift others to success, so that we
may continue making a positive difference in this world.

© 2019 Dragonfly Ranch Consulting

© 2019 Dragonfly Ranch Consulting

CONTENTS

© 2019 Dragonfly Ranch Consulting

© 2019 Dragonfly Ranch Consulting

ACKNOWLEDGMENTS

The nature of this book is to help lift others upward and onward with strategies to assist them with job seeking. All names in this book (besides the dedication and my own) have been changed to protect the identity of the people whose stories have been shared. This book, (and its companion pieces), in no way guarantees job placement.

IMPORTANT: This book has been set up to be a step by step guide on how to use the program. Simply read and do the exercises as laid out and you should be able to kick some major butt by the end of the week on your job search skills and routine!

TO BEGIN:

Take a moment to read the first two chapters of the Blindsided Guidebook. Don't let that freak you out. They are super short and will give you the background information on this program so that you may understand whys and the how of using this program. Plus, they help you pre-plan for Day 1. Trust the process!

AUTHOR'S NOTE:

I highly recommend using this guidebook with the Blindsided: The Video (companion piece). It serves to help you more insight on the practice of this book and the important of frontloading, etc in order to organize your action plan for success.

© 2019 Dragonfly Ranch Consulting

© 2019 Dragonfly Ranch Consulting

"Nothing is permanent in this wicked world.
Not even our troubles."
~Charlie Chaplin

Chapter 1
DUMBSTRUCK

When it happened to me, I was completely dumbstruck. I don't think I ever really knew what "dumbstruck" truly felt like until that moment. You see, I'd heard of people getting laid off, fired at will for no cause, and all sorts of crazy "lost my job" kinds of moments—but it had never happened to me before. Then it did.

I was in shock, sitting in a room that immediately filled with a numbing fog making me feel both "dumb," for not seeing it coming, and "struck" because baby, this was a frickin' blow!

Dumbstruck.

I sat there for moments not quite comprehending what was happening. This kind of thing just doesn't happen to me. I do not fail. I succeed. I am an award-winning, overachiever, top-educator and extremely effective administrator business woman. I have a huge background in public relations, communications and education. I am a connector. I am a promoter of others. I am gawd-damned Michele "FRICKING SUPER SUCCESSFUL AT EVERYTHING SHE DOES" Giacomini. And I got "restructured," (for lack of a better way to explain it). WTF?

I think I went through all the stages of grief within the first five minutes of being summoned to Human Resources that ominous day. Shock. Disbelief. Anger. Sadness. I even did something I thought I'd never do in a workplace. I cried. I felt like such a flippin' wuss. I remember saying aloud "I am not going to cry. Oh screw it, I'll cry if I want. I am upset. I have worked my ass off for this organization and have done an amazing job trying to turn this place (aka: crap hole) around, and now you are doing this? Screw it. I'll cry if I want to." (Besides, it wasn't like it was baseball, right)? So I

© 2019 Dragonfly Ranch Consulting

did, for about a half a second...because anger took back over and that sort of dries up the tears pretty quick.

I got real rationale, real quick as I realized this living nightmare was really real. In a matter of hours I was able to negotiate three different scenarios of change of position, and ultimately, I took the option I thought was best suited for me, and didn't make me look like I was deserting one site & my direct reports, to take some funk-i-fied position at another. Long story short, I left with a "severance package" and a glowing letter of recommendation. (Of course I did—because I was a stellar fricking employee).

But being a stellar employee doesn't necessarily thwart being blindsided when new upper management comes in and decides to change everything.

It doesn't help when there are severe budget cuts that force companies to restructure and lay off.

It doesn't help a top sales manager when he's falsely accused of gender discrimination, just for asking a female employee to work on job improvement.

There are so many reasons people get laid off/let go—but the thing is, it doesn't really matter why. It happened. With or without warning, <u>and you need to move on</u>.

If it has never happened to you before, it's kinda weird. You can easily get stuck in a bit of a funk, not knowing what to do. The deal is, you do not have time to get stuck. You need to strike while the iron is hot and go after your next career adventure.

This guide is about navigating the path to that next adventure. It's not a know-it-all-tell-all book, it's a let-me-help-you-get-off-your-butt-and-get-going-again literary tool.

It's a finding that dang brightside to your blindside, and grabbing life's crappy lemons and squeezing them so hard you make the best darn lemonade of your life! So, that said, let's go over this

© 2019 Dragonfly Ranch Consulting

guidebook and how to use it, because understanding what this tool is about, is key:

- This guide serves to communicate a system about helping you to help yourself get it together and get moving on finding another job. (You have competition out there, so there is not a second to lose)!

- This guide is about showing you many of the components that are important parts of the job search process and how to assimilate them into a working daily schedule, so that you may have the structure to look for resources, leads and ultimately a new job. Keep in mind that everyone is different, so you will need to customize this structure to fit your lifestyle—but also remember that for now, finding your next job IS your job, so make it a priority, as you would any job!

- This guide is for writing in, making notes, brainstorming, you name it. So go ahead, mark it up, notate, dog-ear, whatever you need. USE IT! Besides, the worse it looks by the time you find your next job, just means you have used the heck out of it...so go for it!
(AUTHOR'S NOTE: This is also why you will see the extra margin spacing in the print version—intentionally done so you can make notes in the margins or wherever you want. You're welcome)!

- This guide is big on helping you organize and structure your day. Essentially, you are starting a job of finding a job, and there's a lot to it...and for many people, it is a LOT to learn, real fast.

- This guide is a bit overwhelming AT FIRST, but as you get your routine going and start using all the parts and pieces, it all starts to make sense, and in the long run you will make so much more headway, as a result. The first day of Prep and Day 1 are the hardest, then it is a cakewalk from there on out. You will need to read Chapters 1-4 first, (then you will read one chapter per night for the following chapters, so that you are prepared for what will happen the next day). For the

© 2019 Dragonfly Ranch Consulting

best results, I recommend reading Chapters 1 & 2, then completing the exercises that go with those chapters, then read Chapter 3 and do its exercises, then read Chapter 4 so that you are prepared for all that will actually happen on Day 1. (I realize some of you are chomping at the bit to get going, and that is okay, if you have the time to dedicate today. If not, just follow the suggested reading & exercises/lessons for today of Chapters 1-4, no worries, they are super short chapters). Besides, you may want to have a little lead time to find your office supplies, notebooks, etc that you will need to be ready to hit the ground running on your official Day 1.

Simply put, if you just start reading through the book and taking care of the exercises/lessons as they pop up, you will be doing great!

- After you complete the tasks for Day 1, please read Chapter 5 that evening, to be ready for Day 2 the next day, and so on. We call that "frontloading" in the education/professional development world. It helps you to be prepared for what is coming next. (Try not to read further ahead than that. That's not because of any big surprises lurking later in the book, it's simply so you do not overwhelm yourself more. You are going through a lot. Take a beat and trust this process—it will be enough to digest daily, besides trying to take it all in at once)!

- This guide is also about viewing this horrible thing that happened, (whether it happened to you or a loved one that you are trying to help through this life event), as an adventure. Because that mindframe is more positive, and positivity it's what you need right at this moment. Let's start finding the bright side of your blindside now!

© 2019 Dragonfly Ranch Consulting

"Don't listen to what people say.
Watch what they do."
~Author unknown

Chapter 2
THEY SAID

When it happened to me, people said I'd look back and be forever thankful that this blindside happened. They told me I would be stronger for it.

Well let's get REAL honest about that. I am NOT thankful that my psyche was rocked to its core. Yes, I've learned some things about myself I wouldn't have, had this not happened—but I am not exactly oozing with gratitude for that awful episode in my life. (Maybe I just need more time to get to that point—because when "they" say that, "they" never say WHEN the heck you will actually start feeling that way). What I found is that this Type A constantly-on-the-go personality was suddenly dealing with depression. It's true. A lot of people do not understand that depression is a sneaky bastard and really likes to get ya when you're down. (Yes, that is a joke—gotta lighten the mood somehow, otherwise this is just depressing stuff, right?)

"They" said a lot of things....but there was even more that "they" didn't say.

They didn't say it would take me months and months, (years actually), to wade through the sea of depression from what I considered my first real failure in life. They didn't say I would begin to understand an inkling of what our vets go through with post-traumatic stress disorder. They didn't say I'd wake up at night from nightmares reliving the ordeal for years to come. They didn't say I would be so gun shy once I landed my next job that I was paranoid for months to be "myself" for fear my new employer would think I wasn't good enough. They didn't say it would feel like I had escaped an abusive relationship and that I would live in fear of it happening again.

© 2019 Dragonfly Ranch Consulting

Those aren't fun things, so "they" didn't say anything about that stuff. But I am.

(I know I talked about the "bright side of the blindside," but there is some raw honesty that must be acknowledged first. I want you to know what I discovered through this flippin' nightmare...because it was NOT all rosy and wonderful at the beginning, and I don't want you to think that something is wrong because you aren't feeling chipper about what happened to you). First, it is very normal to feel all of those not-so-fun things and more. You are NOT alone. And if you begin to feel depressed, get help from family, friends and medical professionals. Tell people you are depressed about this situation. (Yes, they probably already know, but there is something about finally vocalizing it, that begins to help lift the weight of depression off your shoulders). So enlist help with dealing with this part—-remember you lost something, and depression is a part of grieving. It's okay to grieve, so you can move on.

Here are some tips on how I got through the depression (keep in mind that everyone is different, so you need to determine what will help you best if you are experiencing depression—and I am NOT a medical doctor, nor a mental health professional, so if you are experiencing depression, be sure to contact one immediately).

- I was fortunate to be able to contact a psychologist through Employee Assistance. If you do not have this through yourself or a spouse, ask your medical practitioner to guide you. You might also contact your local Health Department and ask about local resources you may contact to discuss your depression. Also, there are national resource hotlines to help people who need emotional assistance, such as: https://suicidepreventionlifeline.org/talk-to-someone-now/ Just do NOT delay if you need help—get the help, and get it fast!

- Weight began to lift once I finally admitted to my significant other that I was battling depression. (I wish I would have admitted it immediately to someone, anyone, instead of

© 2019 Dragonfly Ranch Consulting

trying to hide it, because it would have helped me move forward faster).

- I developed a daily "work" routine. Finding work became my new job. Making a list of my daily accomplishments lifted my spirits greatly! (Made me feel like a bad ass at the end of each day, quite frankly)!

- I started reading every business success book I could get my hands on. (Later on, I started looking for podcast interviews with very successful people).

- I started a slideshow of positive memes I came across, a collection of positivity, if you will. Everyday I watched it and added to it as I discovered more. Occasionally, I wrote down my positives and my gratitudes (this was something I now know I should have done more of, to move forward faster). I also created a playlist of empowerment songs. I call it my "Pump Me Up Playlist," and add songs that make me feel confidant, strong and bad-frickin'-ass.

- I reached out to friends I could trust to talk to about my feelings and fears. I was selective on who I shared this information with, and they became a super inner circle of support through this difficult time.

- I listed, listed and listed some more all the things, traits, etc. that I am good at.

- I also listened to the positives "they" said and was realistic that I would also need to deal with the stuff "they" weren't saying while I kicked ass to find a new job. (Aka: Perspective).

(Take a moment to notice that there are a LOT of "I" statements in that list, as well as throughout this book. Why? Because I took accountability for myself and my actions. I am the one who dug myself out of the pit of despair. Did I have help here and there along the way? You bet! But I am the one who chose to put one foot in front of the other, every single freaking day, and kept myself

© 2019 Dragonfly Ranch Consulting

in motion, while I navigated the fog that was trying to envelope me. Because of this, I was able to move forward and into the clear skies of clarity more quickly than my friends and former coworkers who have chosen the route of wallowing in self-pity.)

I believe that you are choosing to also move forward, and propel yourself onward and upward. Soon these "I statements" will be your "I statements," customized for you, of course! That's why you are reading this book right now! Because you are making a positive choice to not let those bastards get ya down! Way to go! You've made the first big step. Good for you!

These are techniques I encourage you to customize and engage in. But the most important is getting help, and finding someone to talk to about the depression, if you are experiencing it. If you aren't, well, good for you, that is truly awesome and I mean that with heartfelt sincerity—but the reality is, many people do become depressed by this sort of life event, and the level can vary from person to person. You really can work through those feelings as you launch yourself forward to finding a new job. So, point being, if you feel depressed, please pause this book for a moment and find help immediately. Then check that off your To Do List, and get back to the book!

JD

I noticed when working with JD he was doing a great job of "holding it together" emotionally during the onset of his unexpected job loss. Considering others I have counselled, I thought he was rather stoic and wanted to understand more about how he was remaining poised.

He shared with me that he had his moments when it was tough, but for the most part, because he had dived in immediately with the Blindsided program, he didn't have time to dwell on the negativity. His daily accomplishments were keeping his spirits high. Plus, by discussing his situation with trusted friends and acquaintances, their feedback was bolstering his confidence &

© 2019 Dragonfly Ranch Consulting

belief that his next career adventure was right around the corner, and he knew he had people keeping him in mind for potential leads.

Most of all, JD also confided that his discussions with those he knew who had gone through something similar, helped him see he was not alone in this unexpected & unplanned for journey.

© 2019 Dragonfly Ranch Consulting

LESSON: DAY 1-WHAT IS YOUR WHY?

After read Chapters **Chapters 1 & 2** of the guidebook, respond to the following:

What is your "WHY"?
Take a moment to think about your "WHY."   Why are you looking for a new job? I know that may seem obvious, but it isn't necessarily. I am asking you to drill down and get to the root of why you are looking for a job. Everybody's why is different. Everybody is unique and in a different place in their life. We may have similar WHYs, but they are all unique to us.

For example, here was mine: My WHY was keeping my home, no matter what. For me, a job meant making money. That was important to me because it meant earning the income necessary to keep my roof, that I love so much, over my head. My children were grown and mostly own their own, financially. No more braces, sports, music lessons or even college tuition to worry about. My biggest concern was not losing the home I had worked my butt off to own (or at least own the mortgage to, right?). Your why could be very different. But we need to know what it is, so you can stay focused on **WHY** you are doing this.

What will a job provide you? (Write it out in this space)

Okay, now that you know what it will provide, <u>why</u> is that important? What do you need it for?

Is that ultimately your 'WHY"? If not, drill down deeper, keep asking yourself "Why?" until you get to the core reason.

© 2019 Dragonfly Ranch Consulting

Once you get there, complete this:

My "WHY" is:

Never forget your **WHY**. This is your motivation. When you have a crappy day and feel super low, come back and read this, so you remember your **WHY**. Stay focused on your **WHY**. Let it drive you. Let it inspire you. Let it motivate you to kick some butt each and every day! We will come back to this shortly, so stay tuned!

Next, read Chapter 3...don't fret...it's short and sweet...but VERY important!

© 2019 Dragonfly Ranch Consulting

© 2019 Dragonfly Ranch Consulting

"Get out of bed.
Work out.
Kick ass.
Repeat.
YOU GOT THIS!"
~Miss OMG

Chapter 3
GET YOUR BUTT OUT OF BED & GET GOING

If you are fortunate enough to be provided a severance package, your new goal is to get a job before it runs out—BONUS POINTS if you can land a new job before you even have to touch it. Some people are not so lucky, and if you are one of those people, your challenge is to find something, anything, to pay for your bare necessities immediately.

So what to do?

Many people advised that I would be out of work for a year. Sadly, they were kind of right that it would take awhile. But I did not let that stop me from starting a "new job" immediately.

Here's how you turn this around on Day 1 of your ~~Lay off~~ NEW JOB ADVENTURE!

First, you need to start a new routine. Now truth be told, the routine you may want to start is to lay in bed for a day or two, maybe even three, and wallow in self-pity. HOWEVER, reality is that every second you hole up hiding, it is a another second that someone else is getting to put themself forward for a new job that could have been yours! So get your booty outta bed and get going!

What I did: (I will outline later again for **YOU**, so just take a moment to absorb this scenario first)

© 2019 Dragonfly Ranch Consulting

My Morning Routine:

1) I got out of bed no later than 7am every morning, and made the bed. (Reason this is important: already productive and a lot less tempting to get back in)
2) I immediately exercised a minimum of 30 minutes first thing (usually 60 minutes—and made up some different daily routines just to shake things up a little)
3) Reviewed My To Do List (Of course on Day 1 I started putting together the initial To Do List)
4) Briefly checked my truly important email
5) Knocked out my Top 3-5 priorities off my To Do List before lunch

My Afternoon Routine:

1) Lunch—20 minute healthy lunch plus a short 10 minute walk (I kinda liked the walking part, so for me, over time I found myself spending less time eating and more time walking when the weather was nice—and on occasion I would grab a sandwich and a water bottle and ate while I walked. Multi-tasking!)
2) Briefly checked my truly important email, again
3) Lists Review
4) Networking
5) Job Searching

My Evening Routine: (This was super hard for me at first)

1) Discovered some hobbies, and engaged in them
2) TALKED (not just emailed/texted) to 1 or 2 friends/family members, made coffee dates, walk & talk dates, tennis dates, etc. to meet with friends in person and chat, to stay connected (and dream together)
3) Went to bed at a normal hour to get a good night's rest

The first day I put this in action, I went to my very best friend's house and we sat in her pool at the end of a long, but productive day. (Luckily, we were still experiencing California Indian Summer

© 2019 Dragonfly Ranch Consulting

in October). I was still reeling from disbelief. She listened, shared some of her own experiences, and then we both began something very positive. We began to dream out loud together. She shared her dreams of writing a children's book, which encouraged me to I confide that I had always been encouraged to write books too. As a former journalist, I had always wished I had time to go back to writing again. We both encouraged each other—and you know what? Six months later, for better or worse, I published my first Miss OMG book. (The fact that I wrote a book in the humor genre, while I was dealing with such emotional distress at the time just baffles me at the irony! But "they" say laughter is the best medicine, right)? The point is, you need to take some time to dream out loud. Explore new ideas, even if they end up only being hobbies, because they can become very healthy outlets.

It is important to get YOUR daily routine together immediately and stay connected to people. Even though you may feel like you are in a fog, just do this. Go through the motions of the routine everyday, NO MATTER WHAT. Soon it will become a comfort to you. Soon you will find excitement to look forward to each day. Soon you will discover that this horrible thing that happened to you has created a new life adventure, and you are on an expedition to find your next job, your next career, your next business venture—whatever the case may be for you—and if you begin to learn some new things about yourself, well that is just icing on the cake!

Vela

When Vela lost her job, she found herself dealing with more than job loss, she found herself trying to cope with overwhelming sadness. So much so, that she spent most of her time hiding out in her bedroom. She shared, "I did not look for a job for 6 months. I just maxed out my credit card and lived off of my parents."

Without support of a career coach or a guide to help her get going again as she waded through her sadness, it took Vela over two months to get a grip on trying to find a new job, and over six months to attain one.

Morale of the story: Stay in motion and gather support. You can do this!

© 2019 Dragonfly Ranch Consulting

LESSON: DAY 1-GET YOUR BUTT OUT OF BED & GET GOING

"Get out of bed.
Work out.
Kick ass.
Repeat.
YOU GOT THIS!"
~Miss OMG

USE PENCIL FOR THIS EXERCISE!
After you've read Chapter 3: **GET YOUR BUTT OUT OF BED &
GET GOING,** respond to the following:
Ultimately, what is your goal in this new career adventure?

Now let's get specific. So, specifically speaking, what does that
mean?

How will you know that you've accomplished this? In other words,
how are you going to measure the success of reaching that goal?

Is that attainable? If not, then go back and change--it's okay! You
may change this a few times...no worries.

© 2019 Dragonfly Ranch Consulting

Now that you have an attainable goal, stop and ask yourself, is it really realistic? Could you realistically attain that goal based on the criteria you have set? If not, tweak until you truly have a reasonable and realistic goal for this job search adventure.

Ok, last, set a time on it. How long are you REASONABLY giving yourself to attain this goal?

Now write out the whole thing:

My goal is to (include the timeframe):

I will know that I have reached it by:

Fantastic! Now you have a SMART goal set for yourself, which means you are setting yourself up for success. WAY TO GO!

Now open up the inside of your spiral notebook/binder. Copy your **WHY** on the inside cover, and then copy your **GOAL**. This will serve as an additional visual for you. If and when you ever doubt yourself, or you are having an off day, open up you notebook and read to yourself. Sometimes we just need a little reminding. (If you

© 2019 Dragonfly Ranch Consulting

are using a 3-ring binder, slip this into a clear window view in the front of your binder so you see it all the time)! I also recommend that you write it on the inside cover of this guidebook...so you always have it handy!

© 2019 Dragonfly Ranch Consulting

Ok, you've got most of your pre-planning done so you can hit the ground running. Now we move on to the nitty gritty.

Day 1: HOW TO GET STARTED WHEN I CAN BARELY START MYSELF? This chapter discusses establishing **YOUR** daily routine.

It is important to get YOUR daily routine together immediately and stay connected to people. Go through the motions of the routine everyday, NO MATTER WHAT.

So go read Chapter 4, then get your supplies together, and get ready to start working on reaching your goals.
This IS happening! You are getting ready to tackle Day 1. (Now keep in mind, the expectation is that you are reading this the evening before you implement Day 1, to prepare yourself...but if you have the day set aside, and want to get started now, go for it)! Let's do this!!!

"For what it's worth,
it's never too late to be who you want to be.
I hope you live a life you're proud of,
and if you find that you're not,
I hope you have the strength to start over."
~F. Scott Fitzgerald

Chapter 4
DAY 1: HOW TO GET STARTED WHEN I CAN BARELY START MYSELF?

You're probably dazed, confused and pretty much not knowing which way is up on your first day without a job. Not to worry, that is what this book is for (even if you lost your job weeks ago). Following these steps will help you put the wheels in motion, even when you may not know which way you are headed. So get ready, because this is a full day!

© 2019 Dragonfly Ranch Consulting

A few things to help you be prepared for the day—first, figure out a system of timers. I use my phone and good ole Google, but others prefer setting a kitchen timer on their desk, while some use their favorite electronic device (artificial intelligence) to remind them. I prefer some sort of AI/phone app so I can set it and forget it and not constantly feel like I need to look at the timer itself—cuz it just wastes, well, er...you know...TIME!

Today will be different than the rest of the week, because today we are working on various components of looking for a job. We are gathering the "parts" for success. (For those of you who were loyal to your last place of employment for eons, this may be a lot of new stuff to take in. Hang in there, and trust the process). All these parts we work on today are critical, and will help you to make lots of headway everyday from here on out.

Be prepared to feel overwhelmed. <u>You should feel that way</u>. I am going to throw a lot at you today. This will be the hardest day, then it all gets easier and easier after today. Here's the deal, we are NOT going to tip-toe into this new job of looking for a job. Tip-toeing is for wimps. You are not a wimp. Right? Right!

You need to be a go-getter, and go-getters go full force with gusto into whatever it is that they are going and getting. So get in that mindset now. You ARE a go-getter, BE a go-getter! Now let's go-get!

You should be so flippin' busy today that you do NOT notice the time and think to yourself, "What? It's ONLY 10am?" Instead, you should be thinking, "OH WOW, it's <u>already</u> 10am, where is the time going?" That's your cue that you are getting into the zone, and that's where you need to be to get back on track!

Get it? Got it? Good.

Now go get your (doctor-approved) exercise in and eat breakfast, because there is no time to break until lunch. Here we go:

© 2019 Dragonfly Ranch Consulting

<u>Day 1-</u>

1) Get an old-fashioned spiral notebook and keep with you at all times (you will use this guidebook you are reading as your resource notebook)...thoughts and ideas are going to hit you at the weirdest times and you need to write them down the second they strike. For today, if you don't have these, use scratch paper until you get to the store or can bum a notbook off someone. (NO EXCUSES)! You can also use a binder with divided sections of binder paper...but you will still need at least a small notebook to keep with you at all times, in case inspiration strikes! (If nothing else, slip a pad of sticky notes into your purse, or several sticky notes into your wallet—just be sure to swap them out when you add those notes to your "real" notebook, as a back-up plan. Don't have sticky notes? Still no excuse—get a piece of copy paper or two and fold them up and slip them into your wallet/purse).

   Also, there is a reason we are NOT doing this technique on a computer—I know it is strange in this day and age, but just trust the process. Studies have proven we are more apt to reach our goals and be more successful if we hand write. (So using old school notebooks are the best method for what we are trying to accomplish).

2) Put together your schedule for the day—WRITE IT OUT! This means skimming through the tasks I have below for you and write them out. I recommend aiming for completing #3-5 before lunch, to the best of your ability, and working on the components for #6 after lunch (I have helped you for the first week-- you will see a condensed version after the narrative version, but next week, you are on you own for writing it out)!

3) Put your Resume on Notice
   It may have been awhile since you've even seen your resume. Find it, dust it off and revamp the hell out of it.

(You will need it IMMEDIATELY for your LinkedIN profile, Indeed and other job search platforms).

Please keep in mind that you need a General Resume and then what I call a "Template Resume" (one that can be customized for special job applications, as needed)

Also, times have changed. A traditional "timeline of jobs" resume is not what people are looking to review. You need to list your skill-sets first, remember employers may get hundreds of resumes for one post, so it is important that your resume passes a paper screening.

(AUTHOR'S NOTE: Just a tip that you will want to get your resume into the hands of friends and colleagues who can deliver it to the hiring managers, VPs, Presidents, etc of companies. This extra effort can make a big difference in getting your resume seen. So make it a priority to get your resume done this week)!

4) Sign-up for Unemployment
Regardless of whether you think you can collect it or not (just in case). The worst they can do is decline your application.

5) Update your Social Media
If you are not on Social Media, today is the day to embrace it. It can be your best friend during events like this: At bare minimum you need LinkedIn and Facebook.

Keep in mind—**do not go on a rant about how you lost your job on your Social Media**—this will turn people off and they will tune you out. There is a difference between posting your hatred of your former company and simply putting out there, "Friends-Was recently laid off and am looking for leads in the blah, blah, blah industry. Please private message me if you hear of anything." People want to help when you are being positive. So, increase

© 2019 Dragonfly Ranch Consulting

your positive frequency, (regardless of how hippy dippy that may sound), and put out good vibes. People like good vibes. They also like funny and happy—even if you aren't feeling so funny and happy at the moment. Search for motivational memes if needed and share them out on your pages. Share positive stories—be a positive ray of sunshine for those to notice. (Plus all that positivity may keep you from burning bridges)!

Clean up your social media and delete anything that you have posted that may not present you in the best light to a prospective employer—because yes, they search you out on your social media. So even if it is legal where you live, delete the hysterical photo of you and your buds smokin' buds. Delete those photos of you doing keg stands. Delete any harsh posts that you may have been spewing in some sort of rage. It is imperative.

Be sure to be a ray of professional sunshine. Do include your posts from your participation in community work or charitable events, etc. Ask friends (behind the scenes) to post public comments of gratitude for how you went above and beyond to help in some sort of generous situation (as long as it is truthful). In other words, paint yourself on social media, in the light of being a stellar human being...and delete anything that could cause questioning by of potential employer.

6) Make lists:
In this guidebook, you will have some lists to fill out. If you need to add even more, feel free to tear out and add to a notebook/binder. This is guidebook will serve as a resource notebook of sorts for you, and as alluded to, we are going to work on lists right now.

First-**NETWORKING/CONTACTS LIST**. Make a list of everybody you know who you might have a

© 2019 Dragonfly Ranch Consulting

possible lead, could keep you in mind for a job, or who would promote the heck out of you if they run into someone seeking a person of your talents. The longer the list the better. (We will go over this a little later when we discuss The Daily 3, so stay tuned). Keep adding daily as you think of people or hear about people you should contact. Think especially about people you know who are networking gurus, super connected, those people who seem to know everybody.

<u>Second</u>-**REFERENCES LIST**. Make a list of 5-10 people you can immediately ask to write you Letters of Recommendation/Reference

<u>Third</u>-**BUSINESS LIST**. Start making a list of businesses, companies, organizations, (places of employment) all around you or where ever you'd be willing to relocate (if necessary). Continuously add to this list—daily if possible!

<u>Fourth</u>-**JOB SEARCH ENGINE LIST**. Make a list of employment search programs: Indeed, ZipRecruiter, GlassDoor, Linked In, EdJoin.org, Temp. Agencies, etc., and register an account for each, if you don't have one already. While LinkedIn presents itself as a social media site, it is actually a great place to go when looking for jobs.

<u>Fifth</u>-**"I TOTALLY ROCK" LIST**. Begin making a two column list:
(<u>Left Side</u>) Your Strengths (What are you good at? It can be anything. Master at Excel, Google Maniac, Marketing Guru, Project Manager Extraordinaire. Whatever you rock at. Stuck on this? Think personal first then: Maybe you are the best peanut butter and jelly sandwich maker in the world—list it, and go from there, if you need to!)
(<u>Right Side</u>) What do you like to do? (Hobbies, pastimes, have-always-wanted-to-do/learn things)

© 2019 Dragonfly Ranch Consulting

7) Now, open a fresh page in your spiral notebook (or binder). This is going to become your **DAILY JOURNAL**. Trust me it's not the froo-froo kind of journal you are thinking of, and it really works. So stay with me, don't check out, this is going to be great—REALLY!

First, make two columns, from top to about the last 2-3 inches of the page.(I just simply draw a line down the center of the page, then a perpendicular line across. It does not have to be perfect, so put your ruler/straightedge away).

1/23 TO DO LIST	TODAY'S ACCOMPLISHMENTS

NOTES:

For the first column you need to list **TO DO LIST**:

Today's won't be as full, but as you think of stuff, write it down.

© 2019 Dragonfly Ranch Consulting

For the second column, list **TODAY'S ACCOMPLISHMENTS**

So let's take a moment right now and do that.

Go back through #1-6 above and bullet key things you were able to do today. Even if it was simply stuff like: "Started Resume Revision," "Began List of Networking Contacts," "Set up Facebook account." That's okay, because it is all progress! You need to see what you were able to get done.

At the bottom of the page, you have written "**NOTES**." This is for important things that have come up during the day that you want to "document" or maybe just not forget. (This sort of Daily Journal is a great practice to get into, even after you find your next job. Because you will be in the practice of writing down your accomplishments, you'll easily be able to share with your future employer the positive contributions you've been making for the company, etc. So keep on writing—besides, the mind can only remember so much. Give your brain a break!)

Now turn the page, and write tomorrow's date, and replicate the template. Now we are going to work on tomorrow's **TO DO LIST,** today:

Go back through #1-6 above again, and this time list everything you still need to accomplish. If it isn't complete, it goes on the list. Now keep in mind, some of the things you've done today are an ongoing process. So if you haven't started a "list" it needs to be on the To Do List. If you have started a list, you'll find it may become part of your daily routine for awhile. You will need to set aside time to review your lists daily (and

© 2019 Dragonfly Ranch Consulting

> always add to them the moment you think of someone/something who/that needs to be added).

This is a busy day, but you can do it—and you kinda have the time now to do it, right? So get going! Jumping right in and being proactive will make a difference—with finding a new job faster and with working through the eratic feelings you may be dealing with. For now, finding a job IS your job. Welcome to working for YOU!

JD

JD was skeptical when he started on Day 1 with "The Lists." He shares, "On the first day I felt like I needed some direction to get started, because I needed a good plan on what to do to get going. But I was also hesitant on what this all (the lists) was about. Once I started using it, and writing out my accomplishments it started showing me the positives and gave me the frame of mind that, yes, I am making progress and getting things completed. It gives the positive self-feedback that I am doing things."

So, it is VERY important, because there are times when you may feel like you haven't accomplished anything, if you don't use this part of the system. He adds, "Some days are better than others, because personal stuff sometimes comes up, so maybe you don't get as much done with the job search, but you're still accomplishing things." It kind of shows you a balance of personal life with job search life.

When it came to the "Daily 3," JD was extremely resistant. His personality type is absolutely adverse to asking for help, and allowing the assistance of a career coach was a huge step itself, let alone being asked to take it a step further and reach out & network.

JD explains, "At first I didn't want to do it. I needed to be coached and encouraged to do this. I don't like reaching out, it's not my personality to reach out and ask for help. But with persistent coaching and guidance, I tried it and found it to be helpful." He shares he discovered some important aspects to this technique,

---

© 2019 Dragonfly Ranch Consulting

"(Networking) led to people giving suggestions, leads, other contacts, and actual support & a willingness to help in anyway they can. It is still hard for me because it pushes my comfort zone." But by doing this he has even experienced some renewed professional relationships. Which is very valuable in both work and personal life.

LESSON: Day 1-To Do List

Now let's put all of this reading together. First, be sure you set up your Daily Journal as the reading suggested. Open up the notebook you have designated as your "Daily Journal." Set up the first page as such:

1/23 TO DO LIST	TODAY'S ACCOMPLISHMENTS

NOTES:

Now add these tasks to your **To Do List** for TODAY:

- Setup your Daily Journal Binder
- Write out your schedule
- Resume Review

© 2019 Dragonfly Ranch Consulting

- Sign up for Unemployment
- Update your Social Media
- Make your lists in second notebook

For each thing you accomplish, cross it off and add it to the TODAY'S ACCOMPLISHMENTS side of the page. While this may seem redundant, there is a reason for this. You are getting into the habit of writing down your accomplishments.
(You will repeat this structure for each page in your Daily Journal).

Next Step, let's set up your schedule for **DAY 1**. It is different than the rest of the week, but stick to it as close as you can. (This routine will evolve over the next couple of days. By Day 4 you will have your solid routine put together). Keep in mind that you are using the details from the guidebook to guide you through the following tasks.

DAY 1 Schedule:

7:00am-	**30 minutes Doctor-approved exercise**
7:30am-	**Breakfast/shower, etc.**
8:00am-	**Getting organized**
9:00am-	**Resume Review & Exercise Lesson**
10:00am-	**Sign up for Unemployment** (you may or may not be eligible, but hey, it's worth a try, right?)
11:00am-	**Update your Social Media & Exercise Lesson**
Noon-	**Break for lunch** (Try to go for a short walk if possible, or get some sort of movement in)
1:00pm	**Create Networking/Contacts List (provided for you)**
1:30pm	**Create Reference List (provided for you)**
2:00pm	**Create Business List** (Places of potential employment) **(provided for you)**
2:30pm	**Create Job Search Engine List (provided for you)**
3:00pm	**Create "I Totally Rock" List (provided for you)**
3:30pm	**Update today's Accomplishments List**
3:45pm	**Set for Success** (Set-up tomorrow's To Do List/Accomplishments Page)
4:00pm	**Read Day 2: Seize the Day**; then take the rest of the day off and **decompress!!!**

© 2019 Dragonfly Ranch Consulting

© 2019 Dragonfly Ranch Consulting

DAY 1 EXERCISES (I know you are reading ahead, but for these exercises, do <u>during your ACTUAL Day 1</u>)

Resume Review:

Take out your resume.

When was the last time it was updated? You might not even have that file anymore! No worries.

Review your resume for accuracy and mark it up. Don't be shy, this is your time to discover what makes you shine.

Circle key titles and tasks. As you think of others, scribble them on the resume.

You need to take some time to also review current resumes styles. Nowadays, key roles & skill sets tend to be listed first, rather than a timeline of jobs/positions held. (Save that for later). Go to the internet and type in **21st Century Resume Templates**. Review and see which ones speak to you. Over the next few days you will update your resume in this fashion.

UPDATE YOUR SOCIAL MEDIA:

1) Take some time to go through your social media platform(s). Review your posts.
2) Do you have any negative posts? Any rants? Anything unsavory or inappropriate in the eyes of a potential employer? TAKE IT DOWN.
3) Next, do you have any photos from positive events (think helping your community, charitable events, etc.)? Be sure to "casually" edit posts to let people know which charity you are helping out, etc. Use your Social Media to put your best foot forward and to shine.
4) Add some positivity images and motivational memes. Not your thing? Make it your thing, **for now**. Potential employers will scour our social media and they want to hire people who are positive and do positive things.

© 2019 Dragonfly Ranch Consulting

CREATE YOUR LISTS:

On the pages to follow are the lists you need to make. Remember, this guidebook is serving as a resource notebook for you, however, you are welcome to pull these pages out and add to a 3 ring binder if that works better for you. Do what feels right for you)!

Here we go! These will be "moving parts" today, but tomorrow, you will put them all together. Think of it as a jigsaw puzzle today, you are just getting the pieces ut and ready to go, and tomorrow you put the puzzle together.

© 2019 Dragonfly Ranch Consulting

NETWORKING/CONTACTS LIST

Make a list of everybody you know who you might have a possible lead, could keep you in mind for a job, or who would promote the heck out of you if they run into someone seeking a person of your talents. The longer the list the better. (We will go over this a little later, so stay tuned). Keep adding daily as you think of people or hear about people you should contact. Think especially about people you know who are networking gurus, super connected, those people who seem to know everybody & add an * next to them.

1. _____	21. _____
2. _____	22. _____
3. _____	23. _____
4. _____	24. _____
5. _____	25. _____
6. _____	26. _____
7. _____	27. _____
8. _____	28. _____
9. _____	29. _____
10. _____	30. _____
11. _____	31. _____
12. _____	32. _____
13. _____	33. _____
14. _____	34. _____
15. _____	35. _____
16. _____	36. _____
17. _____	37. _____
18. _____	38. _____
19. _____	39. _____
20. _____	40. _____

REFERENCES LIST

© 2019 Dragonfly Ranch Consulting

Make a list of 5-10 people you can immediately ask to write you
Letters of Recommendation/Reference

1. _____

2. _____

3. _____

4. _____

5. _____

6. _____

7. _____

8. _____

9. _____

10. _____

© 2019 Dragonfly Ranch Consulting

BUSINESS LIST-Start making a list of businesses (places of employment) all around you or where ever you'd be willing to relocate (if necessary). Continuously add to this list!

1. _____
2. _____
3. _____
4. _____
5. _____
6. _____
7. _____
8. _____
9. _____
10. _____
11. _____
12. _____
13. _____
14. _____
15. _____
16. _____
17. _____
18. _____
19. _____
20. _____

21. _____
22. _____
23. _____
24. _____
25. _____
26. _____
27. _____
28. _____
29. _____
30. _____
31. _____
32. _____
33. _____
34. _____
35. _____
36. _____
37. _____
38. _____
39. _____
40. _____

© 2019 Dragonfly Ranch Consulting

JOB SEARCH ENGINE LIST

Make a list of employment search programs and register an account for each, (if you don't have one already).

1. _____

2. _____

3. _____

4. _____

5. _____

6. _____

7. _____

8. _____

9. _____

10. _____

© 2019 Dragonfly Ranch Consulting

"I TOTALLY ROCK" LIST

LIST YOUR STRENGTHS: What are you great at? What can NO ONE take away from you?	HOBBIES/PASTIMES/STUFF YOU'VE ALWAYS WANTED TO DO:
1. _____	1. _____
2. _____	2. _____
3. _____	3. _____
4. _____	4. _____
5. _____	5. _____
6. _____	6. _____
7. _____	7. _____
8. _____	8. _____
9. _____	9. _____
10._____	10._____
11._____	11._____
12._____	12._____
13._____	13._____
14._____	14._____
15._____	15._____
16._____	16._____
17._____	17._____
18._____	18._____
19._____	19._____
20._____	20._____

© 2019 Dragonfly Ranch Consulting

© 2019 Dragonfly Ranch Consulting

DAY 2 PREP:

YAY! You did it! You got through Day 1. Now take some time to set yourself up for success by reading about Chapter 5 of the Blindsided Guidebook. Keep in mind that the chapters in the guidebook are super short and will provide you the background information on this program and what's to come for the day you are tackling, so that you may begin to understand whys and the how of using this program. As always, trust the process!

"You can't spell 'challenge' without 'change.'
If you're going to rise to the challenge,
you have to be prepared to change."
~Author Unknown

Chapter 5
DAY 2: SEIZE THE DAY!!!
(AKA: Putting all the parts and pieces together day)

Yesterday was hard. I remember my Day 1, and seriously, my brain felt tired by the end of the day. I was dealing with my feelings of anxiety about losing the job I was so attached to, and the surrealness of having to look for a job, (instead of planning a Winter Vacation that week, which was what I had expected to be doing). What a dose of reality! I also was dealing with some tricky aspects of the severance I negotiated. Plus, looking for a job during the time of year I was looking, in my industry, was next to impossible. Regardless, I made a lot of headway that first day. And again, it was hard—so I get it.

I'm not going to tell you that future days won't be as hard, because reality is that life can truly be a kick in the groin. But you are not going to lay on the ground wallowing in pain and self-pity cursing 'til the cows come home. You are going to pull yourself up, dust yourself off and get your butt in gear, again. (And again, and again, and again). Because you are on an adventure here! So let's get ready to tackle Day 2 of this job finding expedition.

© 2019 Dragonfly Ranch Consulting

By now you should have your schedule for today and bazillions of lists already started that I assigned you yesterday. You have set yourself up for success with all the organization you did yesterday. My guess is that you've gotten up at a reasonable time, <u>made the bed</u>, exercised and had some sort of resemblance of a breakfast. Right? Right. (And if you are saying "WRONG" right now, stop, drop and get it together, because you are worth it! You are worth making the effort to have a successful day. You are worthy of the progress you are going to make today. So right your wrongs if you need to, and let's get going—there's no time to waste)!

Now let's do Day 2: Putting it all together

7:00am 30 min. Doctor-Approved exercise
7:30am Breakfast/shower, etc.
8:00am Check your email
- Get in the habit of only checking it 2-3 times per day
- Check at 8am, 1pm and maybe 5pm—spend no more than 30 minutes and <u>set a timer</u> if need be.
- Scan it first for any "important" emails, and respond to those first. If you have time left over in your 30 minute allotment, then respond to other less priority emails, but when time is up, it is up. (Here's the deal, some people may be finding out about your job loss and sending you tons of texts/emails. The words of encouragement are awesome, and yes you need to respond, but it can be a downer and time suck to spend all day doing this. A quick way to wade through this is to send out the following response to every message:

  > *"Hey, thanks for touching base with me. I am trying to wrap my head around all this, as you can imagine. Would really like to chat with you soon and maybe pique your brain for leads, etc. If you have any, please email them to me. I promise I will get back to you sooner than later. Thanks much, talk soon."*

© 2019 Dragonfly Ranch Consulting

Obviously you are going to word it the way you need in order to sound like you.

But you need to stay focused, so this message serves a bunch of purposes:

- It helps friends and family to know you are alive and responsive
- It kindly lets them know you need a little time before talking about the job loss at nauseum
- It lets them know you are already back in the saddle and looking for leads—and it lets them know they can help you by sending you leads
- And, it buys you a little time so that you can get into your new routine of your new Looking for a Job job, so you aren't derailed from your newfound focus

If you end up with extra time today, great! Call them and chat, but not during your "work hours."

A couple tips, if this is a struggle for you:
- Mute the chimes on your email notifications
- Log-off your email all together

8:30am GET FOCUSED & STAY FOCUSED

Get your notebooks—the one for all your LISTS & NOTES (This guidebook), and your DAILY JOURNAL one too (the spiral or binder).

■　First glance over yesterday's journal entry. Take a look at what you accomplished and be proud. Then take a look at Today's To Do List.

■　You need to prioritize the To Do List and get at least the top three most important things on that list done before lunch today.

■　Also, as you accomplish things today, please enter them on today's journal page under, (yep, you guessed it), "Today's Accomplishments."

© 2019 Dragonfly Ranch Consulting

PLEASE NOTE: At times you will have some personal stuff to add to your TO DO LIST. That's okay. But remember to approach this system as a job, and you would not normally be taking care of a bunch of personal things during your "work day," right? If you find that you are, a simple solution is to get up an extra hour earlier everyday and carve out "Personal To Do List Time" during your morning. Another idea is to add that extra hour to your lunchtime to complete personal tasks, or at the end of the day. This way you remain dedicated and focused on your job of job hunting.

Knock out 3-5 of your top priorities on your To Do List (Try to pick the crappiest thing on your To Do List to do first, get it done and then everything else will feel like a cakewalk). NO PROCRASTINATING! Just jump in and get it done! You will feel great as you cross it off and add it to your Accomplishments List for the day.

12:30pm LUNCHTIME-Take 30 and try to decompress (walk or get some sort of movement for 10+ minutes) You really need to stop and take a break. Make yourself. I know it can be easy to get in your zone with all of this and not want to stop, but your brain needs a break—and your body needs nourishment. So stop n' slurp some soup or somethin'!

1:00pm 30 MINUTE EMAIL CHECK
- Stick with the routine: Scan for important emails, then with time left over, respond to those who are checking in
- Thank those who send you leads, and add your leads to your to your lists.

1:30pm LISTS REVIEW TIME (This will become faster as time goes on)
- First review the **NETWORKING/CONTACTS LIST**

© 2019 Dragonfly Ranch Consulting

you've been working on, add anymore that come to mind.

- **TODAY'S TASKS**
  - Search your email address book and add those you've forgotten, if any.

  - Add people from your Facebook, LinkedIn & other social media circles who might be helpful.

  - Think of individuals from your last workplace who you might be able to reach out to.

    IMPORTANT: this becomes part of your daily routine, <u>so do it diligently</u>, add it to your accomplishments, and move on to:

- **SELECT YOUR DAILY 3**

  Your DAILY 3 are the three people you need to contact the most, in order to reach out and professionally holler for help! Start by picking your heavy-hitter, super-connected people. THIS SHOULD BE THREE NEW PEOPLE EVERYDAY. Your message to them should be brief and simple, <u>but also personal</u>. Something like:

  > *"Hey Susan,*
  > *Hope you are doing well.*
  > *How's (blah, blah, blah—insert something sincere and personal here) going?*
  >
  > *I was wondering if you are aware of any opportunities that may be coming available with (such & such company), that might utilize my skills and*

© 2019 Dragonfly Ranch Consulting

talents with (insert what you basically do—ie: Public Relations and Strategic Social Media Marketing)? I am exploring new employment opportunities and would be grateful if you would keep me in mind if you know or hear of anything.

Thanks so much, would enjoy chatting with you when you have some time!

~Michele"

(Be sure to add each person you sent this to, to your Today's Accomplishments, and to your To Do List for a week from today, in order to schedule a Follow-up).

- Next for TODAY, you need to email those 5-10 people you listed on your **REFERENCES LIST** and ask them if they will be references for you, and if they would kindly write you Letters of Recommendation. These letters are very important to some companies/industries. Much like the Daily 3 message, make it brief, but also make it sincere and personal. You can do this quickly by re-using the basics of the same letter, but be sure to personalize it each time! Give yourself 1 hour to get this done...set the timer and GO! (Then add each person you sent to on your Today's Accomplishments list)! YAY!

- Now let's put that **BUSINESSES LIST** to work for the next 60-90 minutes
    Today seek out each company's CAREERS/JOBS section on their website, and BOOKMARK it! If you need to register a

© 2019 Dragonfly Ranch Consulting

profile, do it.

Next peruse it and see what they've got. This takes more time in the beginning, but gets faster as you review daily for any updates

Repeat for each company until your time is up for the day—be sure to add the companies you searched to your Today's Accomplishments List, and the others you will get tomorrow (or if you have a little spare time later today).

- It's time for more Job Searching via the job search engine applications. For the next 60-90 minutes spend your time exploring jobs from your **JOB SEARCH ENGINE LIST**. If you come across new sites, add them to your list so that they become part of your new daily routine.

    Be sure to upload your resume. If it isn't done, try to throw together a slam dunk one for the moment, and then update your resumes in these search engines once you have the final complete. (Keep in mind, these applications usually use a general resume, but occasionally you may need to customize it for various job applications, depending on the site). For example, my resume for Indeed is a broad resume of all my skill-sets, whereas my EdJoin.org resume is customized to highlight my attributes in the education world.

    Be aware that sometimes the search engines that automatically send you leads, may send you stuff you are not interested in at all. Who knows why? Over-sensitive to Keywords, maybe? But review and quickly move on. (You may find some repetition as well, again,

© 2019 Dragonfly Ranch Consulting

review and move on. Also re-check your parameters on a regular basis).

■ **I TOTALLY ROCK LIST**

You are probably wondering why I include this? Well it is simple, these are areas that you may want to add to your resume and your cover letters. Employers want to know that they are getting a quality person with great skills and talents, (and sometimes we need to remind ourselves what in the world those are, especially during times like these). Whatever went down with you and your former employer, that can't take away that you are an incredible: *fill in the blank(s) here*

So for someone like me, they couldn't take away my excellent skills in communicating, organizational strategies & sustainable systems development, high energy, and natural leadership & management by positive motivation abilities. Because at the end of the day, when you strip it all down, that's me. That's who I am.

So who ARE you? What can they never take away from you?

Make sure to glance at this list on a regular basis—(I actually like to glance at it first thing in the morning and last thing for the work day…because it reminds me that I am Michele "Frickin'-Awesome-Super-Successful-at-whatever-she-does" Giacomini, and that my former employer was a fool to ever let me go. Those idiots, their loss...because I'm on an adventure to see who it going to be lucky enough to add me to their team next)! So there. (Yes, it does feel

© 2019 Dragonfly Ranch Consulting

good to say that—rather empowering, actually—I encourage you to try it)!

There is another reason we use the I TOTALLY ROCK LIST, but it comes up in a couple of days and I don't want to ruin the surprise, so hang tight!

5:00pm- Get ready to call it a day.

First, be sure you've written down all your Accomplishments
Second, transfer any TO DOs over to tomorrow's List
If you have any left over time before 5pm, do some more networking:

Respond to people who have reached out to you, or reach out to 1 or 2 more people on your Contacts List.
Third, read the guidebook's **DAY 3: OH MY GAWD, HOW WILL I PAY MY BILLS?**
Fourth, when it is 5pm today, your work day is over. So it is time to play. Look at your **HOBBIES/INTERESTS LISTS**. Is there something on it you can do this evening? Anything you can schedule for later this week or the following weekend? Want to learn to paint? Draw? Something else? Look up YouTube Videos for tutorials. Dust off that book you've been meaning to read. Shoot hoops. Go for a long walk and think about all the positive things you've accomplished today. Be proud. You've got this! (And seriously take the night off—if you suddenly think of something, jot it down in your notebook real quick for tomorrow...in the meantime, go chill out.For a bonus, write down some gratitude or a "bright side" of the day in your notes section.

© 2019 Dragonfly Ranch Consulting

In all, staying positive and looking at your next career or job opportunity as a new and exciting adventure will help to keep up your morale, and keep your eye on the prize of finding your next job. It's all about positive attitude!

Connor

When Connor was laid off in 2013, he took a professional "gap year" to decide what he wanted to do, and spend more time with his family.

When he went back to work, he did so under his owns terms, as a business consultant. He started a new business, and took on project work as an independent contractor. He learned there are good things and bad things about being a subcontractor. First, you call the shots on your hours and terms (to a certain degree), but the drawback is that when your project comes to a close it's often final. The company hired you to do a job, you did it, it's done, and they will let you know if they need your services again for any future projects (which may or may not be on the horizon). This can mean scrambling again to make an income. In a way, it's like knowing with eyes wide open that you will be laid off again on a certain date (but you aren't actually being laid off).

In 2019, Connor wasn't willing to do another "Gap Year," after his project ended. So he got real proactive, real early. He shares, "I immediately went into job search mode & networking with friends, and former co-workers."

After working as an independent contractor for 14 months, he learned some important things about himself. He adds, "My initial reaction to my 'layoff' (contract ending) was acceptance and excitement to start a new job (as an employee) somewhere else, since I didn't enjoy working remote & not having any co-workers based locally."

"My family & friends were my support, I kept up a positive mental attitude with lots of persistence." He continues, "I updated my resume and started researching the latest trends in the Internet industry. I was already looking for new job for last 5 months (of my contract). I didn't take a gap year off since I had already done that after my 2013 layoff. My plan was to apply for anything & everything that I was qualified for no matter which company."

© 2019 Dragonfly Ranch Consulting

As a result of his proactive mentality, Connor has already secured his new position at a new company, as an employee.

(See, I told you it was short)! And just as short is today's lesson...not a bunch of exercises today. Just some roll-up your sleeves and get going on your new daily routine stuff! Feel free to use this area to make notes, cross out, add to, etc on your schedule and get moving)!

LESSON: DAY 2-SEIZE THE DAY!!!

Yesterday all your hard work & organization set yourself up for success.

Today we begin to put all these pieces together.

1) Glance over yesterday's journal entry and be proud of your accomplishments
2) Re-familiarize yourself with Today's To Do List
3) Note that today's schedule is a bit different--stick with it!
4) Refer to the guidebook for the details for each task below

DAY 2 SCHEDULE:
7:00 am/or earlier- **30+ minutes doctor-approved exercise**
7:30 am- **Breakfast/Shower, etc**
8:00 am- **Check your email (set your timer for 30 min.)**
8:30 am-12:30 pm- **Priority TO DO LIST Tasks--Stay focused!**
NOTE: The guidebook has some

© 2019 Dragonfly Ranch Consulting

	priority tasks for you to do today, be sure you add those to your list and get them done!
12:30 pm-	**Lunchtime (Try to get in some sort of 10+ min movement)**
1:00 pm-	**Check your email (set your timer for 30 min.)**
1:30 pm-	**LISTS Review Time**

Start with Networking/Contacts List and make any additions you thought of overnight.
VERY IMPORTANT:
Select your Daily 3 and send a message or call.

References List-Email those 5-10 people and ask for letters of reference

Businesses List-For 60-90 min., seek out the CAREERS tabs on each of your businesses listed, for potential Opportunities. (Remember to bookmark)

Job Search Engine List-For 60-90 min. Seek out job opportunities on various job search engines. Set up profiles and automatic setting for these search engines to forward jobs of potential interest to you (if applicable).

I Totally Rock List-Review your Strengths and add any more that come to mind.

5:00pm-	**Get ready to call it a day.**

First, be sure you've written down all your

© 2019 Dragonfly Ranch Consulting

Accomplishments

Second, transfer any TO DOs over to tomorrow's List

Third, read the guide book's **DAY 3: OH MY GAWD, HOW WILL I PAY MY BILLS?**

Fourth, check out your Hobbies/Interests List and go engage in something fun/interesting/relaxing. Whatever floats your boat! Enjoy the rest of the night!

© 2019 Dragonfly Ranch Consulting

© 2019 Dragonfly Ranch Consulting

DAY 3 PREP:

Day 2 was different than Day 1, for sure. Did you see how all those parts you were gathering were starting to come together? It will become evident and the process will become quicker over the days to come. YOU'VE GOT THIS! Now let's get ready for Day 3. No extra exercises than the tasks prescribed in Day 3, so let's review and get going!

"I make myself rich,
by making my wants few."
~Henry David Thoreau

Chapter 6
DAY 3: OH MY GAWD, HOW WILL I PAY MY BILLS?

Today we need to add a few more things to your To Do List. If you haven't already, you may be starting to freak out about paying your bills. Hopefully, you are in a position that you will be okay and can scrape by for now, or even better. But some of us aren't so lucky. When my husband was laid off from his job of almost 18 years, it took us aback. We had just secured a pool builder, so that obviously was cancelled, and really had to put our heads together on how we were going to "scrape" by on just my salary. That's because we weren't expecting this to happen. (When I finally decided to take a new job, after my "time off," in education, I took a step up in title, but a step down in pay, just so I could sink my teeth into a position I thought I would enjoy). Oops!

Well, you know how "they" say money doesn't buy everything? Well "they" do NOT know what "they" are talking about. Because money pays to keep a roof over our heads, money pays to keep clothing on our backs, and money sure as hell puts food on the table. So that said, there is a lot to be said about money.

So immediately, NOT losing our home was my number one priority, my ultimate goal. It was my "Why." It was my motivation for my husband to find a new job. So I knew I needed to be the best

© 2019 Dragonfly Ranch Consulting

cheerleading resourceful support person possible for him. I mean, I can eat ramen noodles for the rest of my life, as long as I do not lose my home for which I cook those noodles in, ya know? How were we going to do that when we, in matters of minutes were told that we were essentially losing close to 66% of our household income, with no idea of when it would be replenished?

Well, the first thing we had to do was Trim the Fat. Quite frankly, compared to many, we were already living fairly lean. But we did it. It was not easy and definitely was painful, but at the same time, we were keeping our roof over our heads.

Could we have kept a "fatter" lifestyle? Sure! But it would have meant selling our forever home that we had found slightly over a year before.

Could we have given that up and moved in with friends or relatives? Sure. But it was not our goal.

Everybody has their own priorities. You need to figure out what yours are. Your roof may not be your top priority, as long as you have one somehow, someway—and that's okay.

What you need to remember what your "WHY" is. Your motivation for finding new employment. (If you are using this guidebook step-by-step, you already know what this is).

Maybe yours is your mode of transportation, or maybe you are an ultimate minimalist and have zero attachments—that's okay too! (And for you minimalists, I'd really like to grow up and be like you some day—but chances are it will never happen).

So we determined our priorities and set out to carve out chunks of change every which way we could. And if you are like we were and don't have some secret fortune stashed away somewhere, or have a massive trust you can just live off of, then you too may need to trim some fat—and I've got tips for you today as you work through your To Do List.

© 2019 Dragonfly Ranch Consulting

Speaking of which, please add these tasks to your To Do List for today:

- Trim the Fat
- Search Special Groups on Facebook
- Meet-ups
- Seek friends who recently switched careers/got laid off, etc.
- Find an Accountability Partner

So here's your schedule for today, please take some time to tweak it to fit for you. (By-the-way, there is a method to the madness of providing you these daily schedules. Wanna know the rationale? It is simple, I am helping you train yourself to structure your day. You do not have time to squander a day spinning on one thing, or even worse—doing nothing. Having a structured day is a great coping method as well. It sets you up for success, you accomplish more and at the end of the "work day" you feel good about being productive. So the sooner you get used to setting up a daily routine and schedule out your priorities, the faster you'll be on the road to success. Oh, and remember make your bed and exercise first thing)!

Let's do DAY 3-	
7:00 am/or earlier-	**30+ minutes doctor-approved exercise**
7:30 am-	**Breakfast/Shower, etc**
8:00 am-	**Check your email (set your timer for 30 min.)**
8:30 am-	**DAILY AGENDA REVIEW/PRIORITY TASK TIME** (To Do List) Review yesterday's Accomplishments & Today's To Do List. Prioritize the To Do List and get at least the top three most important things on that list done before lunch today Remember to note Today's Accomplishments as you check off

© 2019 Dragonfly Ranch Consulting

your To Do List

8:45 am-   **TRIM THE FAT**

Saving money is making money right now. Go through your checking account, look at your auto pays, check your credit cards. (After today, make this a weekly thing—Fridays can be an especially good day, before the weekend comes to entice us to spend—it's like a little reality check before we go blowing a bunch of moola on a weekend of fun). The objective is to pare down to the essentials, so that you don't have debt, or you have very little. Here are some ideas to get you started:

- Look for expenditures you really can cut back on. Do you need a wine of the month membership right now? Weekly housekeepers? Do you need a full blown television package when you can get by on free/inexpensive internet options? Do you really need that subscription radio service? Look for things/memberships you can cancel for the moment. It adds up. Many places will let you pause a membership for case such as these, without penalty. So ASK!

- Look for necessary expenditures that could be downgraded to save money (phone plans, deluxe garbage service, food/grocery delivery, etc.)

- Look up the people who owe you money and tell'em it's time to pay it back

- Want to hang out with friends but need to pull in the reins on spending? Game Nights are a great way to

© 2019 Dragonfly Ranch Consulting

have a bunch of fun without spending money. Rotate at each others' places, and do the ole potluck & BYOBeverage thing. Low cost fun!

- Date Nights do not need to cost anything. Get creative and come up with fun things to do that are free, or are very close. These sorts changes may even stay with you long after you find a new job— saving you a lifetime of money!

- Got a life insurance policy? Some people have policies that can be borrowed against. Not sure? Call and ask your agent.

9:30am TEMPORARY INCOME-Look for ways to bring in additional income. Make it a "game." This week your goal is to figure out how to legally make an extra $50 a day, next week $75 a day, or whatever your want your escalating goal to be. It gets the entrepreneurial juices flowing, and it helps you pay the bills and eat, so there's always that bonus, too. Anytime you do not have to tap into savings or a severance it is a good thing.

- Did you sign up for Unemployment? If not, do it NOW. It's not a guarantee, but nothing ventured, nothing gained

- Turn in your recycling for cash (if you can do that where you live)

- Check out what people are giving away on Craigslist, Marketplace, etc, that you could pick-up for free and turn around and sell

- Check out freelancing sites

- Check out Temp. Agency Sites

- Ask friends and family if they have some odd jobs you could do for them

© 2019 Dragonfly Ranch Consulting

- Are you in a position to rent out a room in your home? Can you possibly move somewhere temporarily & legally sublet your place?

- Look into working as a food delivery person, etc.

You get the picture. Another thing you could do is ask friends about unique side gig work they may know about. Ask, ask, ask! Don't be too proud. Think of it his way, if you can do some side work for friends or family, you could actually list them a reference and they could truly & honestly attest to what a great employee you are—so double win!!!

10:30 am TO DO LIST—Work on your other top priorities

12:30 pm LUNCHTIME-Take 30 and try to decompress

1:00 pm   30 MINUTE EMAIL CHECK

1:30 pm   NETWORKING
- Review your **NETWORKING/CONTACTS LIST** and determine who your Daily 3 are for the day and contact them (FOR TODAY, SEEK OUT 3 PEOPLE WHO YOU KNOW WHO WERE MORE RECENTLY LAID OFF OR WENT THROUGH A CAREER CHANGE. Don't know anyone like that? Then be sure to ask your Daily 3 if they know anyone you could touch base with who has gone through a similar situation. Follow-up with those people right away). Comparing notes with others who have gone through a similar experience is a great way to learn from others' mistakes and their best practices; thus, saving you gobs of time!

  One thing you need to ask these people is if they hired a Labor Attorney, and if so, do they have any recommendations? If possible, consider consulting with a Labor Attorney about your lay off/severance

© 2019 Dragonfly Ranch Consulting

package (or lack thereof), etc. and see if you have a case for a strongly worded letter, (or more) to increase any benefits possible (more weeks of severance, etc.). (You may not have any grounds for any legal action, but at least if you ask, you will know. Some attorneys may offer a free initial consultation. Further, if you have access to Employee Assistance, especially through a spouse, you may be eligible for a free consultation. Seriously, ask your local library if they have any referrals for free legal advice.)

- Next, get on Facebook and search special interest groups related to work/finding work and ask to join those groups.

- Finally, go to Meet-up.com and look for similar special interest groups and RSVP to attend a meeting. These don't have to be all professional, either. Joining large interest group meet-ups affords an opportunity to meet more people and network. Put those meetings on your calendar and be sure to go!

3:00 pm JOB SEARCHING

- Spend the rest of your "work day" searching for new jobs online. Be sure to check out the employment tabs on the internet for the companies you have listed on your **BUSINESS LIST** and the listings your **JOB SEARCH ENGINEs** have sent you. (Basically, whenever you can set up job search engines to automatically send you listings do it! It will save lots of time).

4:45 pm ACCOUNTABILITY PARTNER-FIND ONE!

You may notice that you still have "Accountability Partner" on your TO DO List. Having an Accountability Partner is a great success strategy and can be used for all sorts of life goals. (Finding a new job,

© 2019 Dragonfly Ranch Consulting

weight loss, fitness, project completion, etc.) When you know you need to answer to someone about your progress, you tend to hold yourself more accountable to make real progress—which often leads to greater success.

An Accountability Partner, in this case, is someone who you can count on to check in with you daily to see how you are doing, to inquire on your progress and daily accomplishments. Someone to share how your Daily 3 discussions went, to be a sounding board, etc. You need to select someone to be this person for you. (You may even want to ask him/her if they would like you to reciprocate on some sort of goal he/she is working on). WIN-WIN!

For me, this person was my husband, and visa versa when he lost his job. Each day I would check with him on how things were going. I would ask him to share the highlights of his accomplishments with me. I'd ask him who his Daily 3 were and what transpired when he connected with them. I would ask if he added anything new to his Job Search List or Business List. You get the picture. As his Accountability Partner, I was the person he held himself "accountable to," because he knew each and every day I was going to ask for his recap of the day, and he knew he needed to have authentic stuff to report.

I still have Accountability Partners who I work with on a weekly basis, for various projects I am working on. We reciprocate by checking in on each other to see how each other's week is going, finding out what sort of progress we've each made and what the next

© 2019 Dragonfly Ranch Consulting

steps are for the following week. We also are there to bounce ideas off each other. It is not a competition, it is a total circle of support. Even when we are working on our own projects, we keep each other in mind in the event we come across something that might benefit the other person. Together we are more successful, as a result of our weekly accountability check-ins.

5pm Get ready to call it a day!
Review today's accomplishments and tomorrow's To Do List.
Then, read **DAY 4: LET'S GET RESOURCEFUL.**
- Time to go do something fun or relaxing. Take the time to do this! It helps your brain have a break, and can often lead to great inspiration. You've worked hard today, so give yourself the evening off, or go meet up with some of those friends you've been meaning to get back to.

© 2019 Dragonfly Ranch Consulting

Get it? Got it? Good! Now that you understand the ins and outs of Day 3's To DOs, here's a simplified version of the schedule. You will need to start writing out your own schedule next week, but for now, I'm saving you time and helping you get used to the format, by doing it for you:

Day 3 Schedule:

7:00 am/or earlier-	**30+ minutes doctor-approved exercise**
7:30 am-	**Breakfast/Shower, etc**
8:00 am-	**Check your email (set your timer for 30 min.)**
8:30 am-	**DAILY AGENDA REVIEW/PRIORITY TASK TIME** (To Do List)

Review yesterday's Accomplishments & Today's To Do List.
Prioritize the To Do List and get at least the top three most important things on that list done before lunch today (which are the tasks added for today, refer to the guidebook for details)
Remember to note Today's Accomplishments as you check off your To Do List

8:45am-	**Trim the Fat**
9:30am-	**Temporary Income**
10:30am-	**Other To Do List Tasks**--Work on your other top priorities now
12:30 pm-	**Lunchtime (Try to get in some sort of 10+ min movement)**
1:00 pm-	**Check your email (set your timer for 30 min.)**
1:30 pm-	**Networking Time (Daily 3)**

(FOR TODAY, seek out 3 people who more recently were laid off/went through a career change). Pay close attention to the other networking tasks to accomplish today, from the guidebook. These are very important strategies for 21st Century job searching

© 2019 Dragonfly Ranch Consulting

3:00pm-	**Job Searching**
	Spend the rest of your "work day" searching for new jobs Online, using your Businesses/Job Search Engine Lists.
4:45pm-	**ACCOUNTABILITY PARTNER-**
	Find one!
5:00pm-	**Get ready to call it a day.**

> **First,** be sure you've written down all your Accomplishments
>
> **Second**, transfer any TO DOs over to tomorrow's List
>
> **Third**, read the guidebook's **DAY 4: LET'S GET RESOURCEFUL; (then go play)!**

© 2019 Dragonfly Ranch Consulting

© 2019 Dragonfly Ranch Consulting

DAY 4 PREP:

Here we go, this next part will get you ready for Day 4, so no time to waste, let's get right to it!

"A resourceful person will always make opportunity fit his or her needs."
~Napoleon Hill

Chapter 7
DAY 4: LET'S GET RESOURCEFUL

There are so many resources out there to help you along the way of getting back on track.

- One of the the things I highly recommend is making sure your library card is updated for your local library. There are many FREE reasons I mention this. First of all: audible books. I didn't have a coach to help me get back on my feet, it was all on me, but I did surround myself with many pseudo-literary coaches, if you will. I started "reading" every single business how-to book I could find through my local library. The beauty is, I was able to download and listen to these books everyday while I exercised, and again during my stretch breaks throughout the day. This helped me tremendously. Why? Because I was able to glean new strategies, techniques and insight from those who have already blazed a successful path in life. Most of all, instead of going to the dark side and letting my deep-seeded negative thoughts surface and hijack my day, I was listening to powerful and positive voices imparting their wisdom as I cycled & walked during my exercise sessions; thus, amping myself up with great endorphins and positivity from top to bottom. (Hey, don't knock it 'til you try it—it may work for you too)!

  I also highly recommend getting in touch with your local libraries because some often have information on workshops

© 2019 Dragonfly Ranch Consulting

for adults trying to update their resumes or brushing up on their interview skills, etc. I cannot speak for all counties, but the one I live in has the hook-up on some inexpensive Adult Education classes to learn basic computer skills, social media skills, Excel, PowerPoint, etc. So if you are in need of learning some 21st Century Skills fast, check with your local library.

- Something that is very important for you to do is to go through your email (hopefully you still have access to your former work email, but you may not). Look for positive remarks and recognitions from people about your performance. PRINT THESE OUT. This serves a few different purposes. First, it can help jog your memory on some of the projects, etc. you've worked on that you might be able to add to your resume. Second, it can help with examples to add to cover letters when applying for jobs. Third, it can remind you of people who you may be able to use as a reference or ask to write you a letter of recommendation. Of course there are many others good reasons to do this, but another important one is it feels good too!!! And we all need a little positive pump-up now and then—and NOW is definitely a good time! Right?

- Another area to check for chunks of awesomeness is on your evaluations. ALWAYS keep copies of these in a file at home (even better, scan them and send them to your personal email). Skim through those and be sure to add important highlights to your resume. (Most of all, making a list of these attributes will help boost your confidence, especially for the interview process, and keep your mind fresh on different things you do best).

- Along these lines, a dear friend reminded me that one of her tips is to go back through projects, etc. to review the financial impact (what you were able to help save or how much you were able to make for the company). If this applies to you, this also bodes well for talking points in both cover letters (when applicable) and definitely during interviews.

© 2019 Dragonfly Ranch Consulting

- When you are working through all these different areas, it may spark some other ideas for you to mine more golden nuggets of your personal achievements. So, be sure to keep a list of goals you have achieved. (The I TOTALLY ROCK List could help house these). Also, many areas of how you were able to solve problems may come to mind. Write those down. Again, these are often key points that you may need to reference shortly, so make a list in your notebook!

Something to learn from this is that if you haven't already, from here on out you need to be keeping a KUDOS file, both physically and electronically. Print out those pieces of positivity, and also be sure to forward copies to your personal email and store in a little file in the cloud. Just set up a little folder in your personal email and label it something fun, like: PICK-ME UPS, or IMSOAWESOME, or KUDOS2ME, or whatever floats your boat. Just be sure to do it, so you are never in a situation again where you are sifting through emails trying to find past made accolades.

© 2019 Dragonfly Ranch Consulting

So, for Day 4, add to your To Do List:

LOOK FOR POSITIVE COMMENTS, ACCOLADES, etc.

Ok, here we go, onward and upward for Day 4-
(Did you make your bed and exercise? And NO, I am not going
to let you off the hook on that!)

7:00 am/or earlier-	**30+ minutes doctor-approved exercise**
7:30 am-	**Breakfast/Shower, etc**
8:00 am-	**Check your email (set your 30 min. timer)**
8:30 am-	**DAILY AGENDA REVIEW/PRIORITY TASK TIME** (To Do List)
	Review yesterday's journal of accomplishments & Today's To Do List. Prioritize the To Do List (& always notate today's accomplishments as you complete them), with this new addition on top: **LOOK FOR POSITIVE COMMENTS, ACCOLADES, etc.**
12:30 pm-	**LUNCHTIME**-Take 30 to eat & rejuvenate
1:00 pm-	**30 MINUTE EMAIL CHECK**
1:30 pm-	**NETWORKING**
	Daily 3 Social Media interest/networking groups (Facebook, LinkedIn, Meet-up, etc.)
3:00 pm-	**JOB SEARCHING**
	Review Business List and continue searching for jobs on-line
4:30pm	**Accountability Partner Time** (you may need to customize when this happens, but be sure to squeeze it in somehow) Reciprocate for each other: what went well today, tomorrow's goals/priorities, next steps
5pm	**Get ready to call it a day.** **First,** be sure you've written down all your Accomplishments

© 2019 Dragonfly Ranch Consulting

> **Second**, transfer any TO DOs over to tomorrow's List
> **Third**, read **DAY 5: OUT OF THE BOX THINKING**
> **Fourth,** (go play)!

(Did you notice the schedule is getting easier? It will continue to do so as you knock out more and more priority tasks. YAY)!

So today was all about being resourceful. Resources can come from all sorts of places and people. You never know when someone you meet is going to lead you to your next career adventure.

Chuck

When Chuck. lost his job, his initial focus was on getting back in the game purely to show the people who "wronged him" by letting him go, that they would not win.

He shares, "I came from a small, fairly incestuous industry and found it difficult to break back in, as there were people who I had to part ways with in the past that were now at competitors." He continues, suddenly "I realized it would not be the easiest landing and started to look for things outside my industry and wanted to look at any opportunity."

So what to do when you're in your 40s and can't even remember working in any other industry?

In Chuck's case he started thinking about getting help, and he certainly wasn't ruling out hope for a divine intervention.

© 2019 Dragonfly Ranch Consulting

"There is a saying that God works in mysterious ways and I wanted to open to His call or at least what I perceive to be His call," explains Chuck. "I had been peppered with email by franchise brokers." So he decided to talk to one who pitched some concepts. But Chuck said something didn't feel quite right with that broker.

He didn't give up. Instead he went to a presentation by another broker given at his outplacement assistance center. Chuck confides, "I could tell this broker had her act together. She didn't promise big dreams she just said you don't need to invest a million dollars to get a good business set up." That set well with Chuck so he began consulting with the broker after their initial meeting.

"Going through this I realized that I had been wanting to do this for a few years, (not be out of work), but make an investment for some passive income." He adds, "We settled on a personal services business because you can't be put out of business by Amazon or China with that type of business."

Now Chuck and his wife have just recently debuted their new business. Chuck has also accepted a new full-time position at a new organization. But now being a business owner, he believes he has more choices. He's calling the shots on his future, and he's quite okay with that.

DAY 4 EXERCISES

LOOK FOR POSITIVES, POSITIVE COMMENTS, ACCOLADES, & OTHER SET YOURSELF UP FOR SUCCESS EXERCISES

© 2019 Dragonfly Ranch Consulting

There are so many resources out there to help you along the way of getting back on track. Surround yourself with success and positivity.

Books/podcasts: Make a list of the next 5 success books/or podcasts you plan to listen to (or actually read)!

1. _____

2. _____

3. _____

4. _____

5. _____

Where is your nearest local library?

_____

What is the library's phone number?

_____

Now call them and ask if they have any adult job search workshops/work skills enhancement workshops, etc. Do they know of any job search resources? Networking groups?

What was the name of the librarian you spoke to?

_____

© 2019 Dragonfly Ranch Consulting

NEXT: Scour your address books/email & phone contacts lists/(your old rolodex, LOL!), and add these people to your Networking/Contacts List

How many people were you able to add to your Networking List from this exercise? _____

Scour your emails for positive comments from supervisors, co-workers, clients, etc. (especially if you can legally get access to your former work email). If not, be sure you always print these out in the future! If you can't access, think back to times when you received KUDOs. What were they for? List the areas that people praised and thanked you for your help/talent/skills, etc.:

1. _____

2. _____

3. _____

4. _____

5. _____

Evaluation time! Find your past evaluations and go through them. List your top 5 glowing remarks about you below:

1. _____

2. _____

3. _____

4. _____

5. _____

Feeling awesome? You should!

© 2019 Dragonfly Ranch Consulting

FINANCIAL IMPACT-Next, think about if there were times that you saved your previous employers money? Were you ever assigned to any projects? If so, what was the financial impact for the company, as a result of your hard work? Take a moment to think through those. Sometimes you may have been able to save a company time or manpower for a job; what financial amount did that equate to?

Write out your notes on this here:

GOALS ACHIEVED-List any newfound golden nuggets of your personal achievements you have discovered on your **I TOTALLY ROCK LIST** under **Strengths.** This helps serve as a central point of highlighted accomplishments that you may refer to when drafting a cover letter or prepping for a future meeting or interview.

Next, keep a list of goals you have achieved and/or any problems you were able to solve for your previous employers. Write those down on your Strengths List.(If you need to add an extra sheet or two in your notes for this, then bravo, go for it)!

Now that you have finished this, go back to your To Do List, to take care of your next set of priorities for the day.

DAY 5 PREP:
On day 5 we explore Out of the Box Thinking. By now, you should be putting together a solid schedule for yourself and seeing the

© 2019 Dragonfly Ranch Consulting

benefits of hitting the various components. But today, I also want you to revisit your "**I TOTALLY ROCK LIST.**"

Take a look at the more "professional" skills you listed. Circle the top 5-6 that you just absolutely LOVE doing (or at least enjoy to a certain degree).

Now write them out here:

_____

_____

_____

_____

_____

_____

© 2019 Dragonfly Ranch Consulting

When looking at just this list, what sorts of jobs come to mind.
Pretend a friend with these skills above was asking you to
brainstorm what sort of jobs he/she could apply for with those skills.
What would you advise?   Write them down:

_____

_____

_____

_____

_____

_____

_____

_____

_____

© 2019 Dragonfly Ranch Consulting

Ok, with this list of potential jobs, that utilizes skills that you enjoy, which industries employ people for these positions? You may only think of one or two, but over the weeks to come, as you are reaching out to your Daily 3, ask each person their thoughts. You may discover an industry you never thought of before!

_____

_____

_____

_____

_____

For each of these industries, take some time during your Businesses Lists part of your day and explore industry search engines.

Next, add to your To Do List for next Monday, to search the internet for some sites to explore industries. Vault.com as a great section, and so does the United States Department of Labor with their Occupational Outlook Handbook, and CareerOneStop has a bunch of great information for career comparisons, etc.

You should also look for sites that have career assessments. One of my favorites is MyNextMove.org. It has a great Interests assessment to get you started. BE HONEST when you complete the quiz. I really like their industry browse section, as well. I also use the key areas determined by the Interests assessment to plug in to their Search Careers section a and was surprised by the positions that utilize my interests.

Now that you are movin' and groovin', let's explore some Out of the Box Thinking tips in Chapter 8:

© 2019 Dragonfly Ranch Consulting

"Believe in yourself, listen to your gut, and do what you love."
~Dylan Lauren

Chapter 8
DAY 5: OUT OF THE BOX THINKING

Following are some suggestions for you to possibly try. These are a bit "out of the box," so some ideas may resonate with you, or maybe all, (or maybe none). The point is to get your creative juices flowing to help spark ideas of helping you to stand out in a crowd of applicants.

YOU SHOULD'VE BEEN IN PICTURES-One of my favorite "out of the box" tips was shared by a good friend when my husband lost his job. She mentioned she knows someone who puts together her own customized video presentations and sends them to companies she is interested in working for, without there even being a job posting. (Did you know most jobs that are available out there aren't even posted? Yup. That IS a shocker, so this is a great way to get your foot in the door.) This gal helps companies see why they need to create a position for her, and how she would be such an asset for their company.
'

PUT YOUR HEADS TOGETHER-Find one, two or three people who may be looking for work as well, or who may be considering a career change. Schedule a weekly "meeting of the minds" to discuss job searching aspects, resources, leads and whatnot. Maybe divide and conquer on reading business books, articles, etc. and have each person read a different one each week and present key points they learned from those books/articles at the next meeting. Regardless of your meeting agenda, be sure everyone stays on point, nobody monopolizes the whole meeting and that everyone walks away feeling like it was productive. Remember, this is a <u>collaboration</u> method. (Take this an extra step farther and possibly agree to also be each others' Accountability Partners).

TOOT YOUR OWN HORN-Create a very short video as a brief interview of yourself. Think of it as a "what you see is what you get"

© 2019 Dragonfly Ranch Consulting

pitch of sorts that explains why you are an asset to an organization. (This is different from the deliberate presentations mentioned above). Then upload this to YouTube, and add the link to your cover letters, and your resume. This is a unique way of allowing prospective employers a personal glimpse at who they would be interviewing. Keep in mind that you need to be professional, but not stiff and cold. Be warm, inviting and confidant. (Also be sure that you have a squeaky clean YouTube account)!

BE YOUR OWN MARKETING TEAM-Create an ad with a link to your personal professional website, highlighting yourself and your attributes, (as well as your resume). Then engage in strategic advertising via Social Media to target the industries you are trying to attract. Don't have a personal professional website? Most people don't, unless it is a blog. So develop one (not a blog, just a personal site). Or at minimum, create a page and publish to the web so that it can be accessed via link. A simple page with a brief bio and your resume will do.

FLIP YOUR PRESENCE AT JOB FAIRS-While Job Fairs are not "out of the box," finding a way for standing out at one definitely presents a challenge! Prospective employers establish a presence at these events, in order to do two things: 1) Meet a mass amount of people quickly who could be possible candidates for upcoming positions, and 2) Public Relations (making sure they are demonstrating they are a strong company that people should want to work for, etc.) So essentially, a Job Fair is a See & Be Seen event for all intensive purposes. That said, you need to attend these with the same mentality. So what is your plan of attack to get noticed and be remembered?

In addition to your resume, you should have some business cards printed up. There are online companies that can do this very inexpensively. (And they are very handy to keep on you at all times—you never know who you will run into, and where)! Be sure you choose a more unique style of card...but don't go dorky. Remember, this is a tool that is representing you! I recommend a couple things with style: If possible order a card with a non-traditional shape: square or maybe a circle. Also, you want the card to be a golden rod type color (red is also very noticeable—but

© 2019 Dragonfly Ranch Consulting

can be a little "too in your face" depending on how it is designed). On these business cards you should have a link to your personal (professional) website (for which you will already have your resume on), as well as the link to the video intro you made and put on YouTube. Splurge a bit and add a backside to your card that lists your greatest skill-set strengths. Make sure your font size is 12pt or larger to make it easier for others to read, and your name should be about 2 pts larger than whatever other size you make the rest of the text. When handing this card out, be sure to mention your name & be sure to mention your links on the card. (It's a memory thing, just go with it). At events like job fairs, you want to help the recruiters from the various businesses to remember you. So be sure to do a few more things to help them remember you and your name:

- Bring a name tag, just in case there aren't any. Whenever possible write your name in dark blue ink and use a red pen to make a box around your name. VERY IMPORTANT: Always wear your name tag on your right side. The reason is simple: people tend see it and remember it more because we tend to shake hands in our culture when meeting people, and we shake with our right hand. Therefore the eye tends to view to the right when shaking hands. (Great "ah ha moment" right? You're welcome!)

- While shaking hands, give a sincere compliment: "Hi! I am Michele Giacomini, it is very nice to meet you, and I just need to tell you (lean in slightly here) I have been admiring your earrings." (Or compliment a color they are wearing or their shoes, etc. but make sure you mean it). Even better, whenever possible, if you know something about that person, use a more personal compliment: "Hi! I am Michele Giacomini, and I am thrilled to meet you. I read your article on LinkedIn about (blah, blah, blah)."

- If you can get a conversation going, that could really work to your favor. Try to "naturally" find something you have in common and think of something (ie:. info on the topic you are discussing) you can offer to send the person at a later time, via email, or something that they could send you via email, etc. The thing is, you are trying to have an excuse to

© 2019 Dragonfly Ranch Consulting

write something on your business card...because it gives the person another reason to remember you. Your excuse for writing on the card should be something like, "If you don't hear from me by Monday, please zip me an email." Hand it to the person and THEN say, "Even better, do you have a business card?" Most likely they do, so take it, and right in front of them, write on the card "Email (blah, blah, blah)." This will help you to remember who that person was when you are going through your cards later, and it gives you an opportunity to contact them again (and they are going to remember you, because they will recall you were going to email them about the blah, blah, blah you discussed).

- Another little tip is to wear something very unique. That doesn't mean wear a clown suit! Dress professionally, but wear an interesting brooch/lapel pin. Why? Because it may give the recruiter an opportunity to comment on it, thus, helping them to remember you even more! (And yes, wear it above your name tag. Just another strategy for the Name Game).

- After the Job Fair is over, make sure you take the time to send personalized thank you notes to the recruiters. (Hopefully you have that extra special something you promised to get back to them on, or you were going to check with them about). Regardless, take this opportunity to thank them for the time they spent chatting with you. You will want to reiterate your conversation, let them know that after much thought, you realized you walked away very interested in exploring opportunities for employment at their organization, and ask a question or two, in order to spur on-going communication.

If any of these Out of the Box techniques resonate with you, or help spark a different idea, be sure to write them down and add to your To Do List. If not, no worries, just let them marinate in the back of your mind. You may not follow of any of these, but the hope is that in the back of your mind, you begin brewing some unique ideas of your own!

© 2019 Dragonfly Ranch Consulting

Are you ready for Day 5? You should be! You are doing great. By now you've been putting one foot in front of the other. You are moving forward, despite any feelings you may have toward the worklife you just had yanked out from under you. SO BRAVO!!! Keep it up! And anytime you think you are not making progress, stop and get out your accomplishments journal and review the day or the week and see how much you have done. It's a lot more than you may be giving yourself credit for, so pat yourself on the back and keep on, keepin' on!

© 2019 Dragonfly Ranch Consulting

Now let's take Day 5 by storm: (You've got this. And YES, I know you made your bed and exercised already—so I am not going to even ask, because I trust you)!

7:00 am/or earlier- 30+ minutes doctor-approved exercise

7:30 am- Breakfast/Shower, etc

8:00 am- Check your email (set your 30 min. timer)

8:30 am- DAILY AGENDA REVIEW/PRIORITY TASK TIME (To Do List)
(Remember, worst for first)!
Today, for your Top Priority, add **Day 5 OUT OF THE BOX THINKING EXERCISES**. Then do them, and then return to your other top priorities.

12:30 pm- LUNCHTIME-Take 30 min. to eat & rejuvenate

1:00 pm- 30 MINUTE EMAIL CHECK

1:30 pm- NETWORKING
Daily 3
Social Media interest/
networking groups (Facebook, LinkedIn, Meet-up. etc.)

3:00 pm JOB SEARCHING
Review Business List and continue searching & APPLYING for jobs on-line

4:30 pm Accountability Partner Time
Reciprocate for each other: what went well today, tomorrow's goals/priorities, next steps

5:00 pm Get ready to call it a day.
First, be sure you've written down all your Accomplishments
Second, transfer any TO DOs over to tomorrow's List
Third (go play)! (Reading the last of this book is a great option, or save it for tomorrow, your choice)

© 2019 Dragonfly Ranch Consulting

With "out of the box thinking" comes a chance to meet others who have found a way to make a living, and for some, much different than they intended! Be sure to talk to people about their journey. Discuss with store owners how they started their businesses, ask successful friends about their paths. You will probably discover that all the paths taken had their struggles, but by seeking out these people and learning from them, and the risks they took, you may find yourself very inspired!

Max

Max didn't know what to expect when he decided to create his own safety net of job security. He was working for a company that suddenly found themselves failing at a rapid rate, after 60 years of business. Max knew it was time to get a side hustle going, and fast!

Luckily, Max had many years of pool building experience from his years before entering corporate America. So he and his wife decided to go for it.

"Owning my own business was scary at first. You don't 'know' if it will succeed and there is a ton of pressure on you to make it happen," shares Max. "My wife was the biggest support and I couldn't do it without her. My new career path aligns more with my life goals than corporate America did. Freedom to spend more time with family (kinda ha,ha), set my own schedule, and of course financially it has been an improvement. It also opens up other business opportunities."

So knowing that they were jumping into this adventure together, helped Max with the support he needed, which built his confidence, as well.

"The goal of my business was a 'side business,' but also a safety net to fall back on." Max says that if you are going to build a business, there are some things you should consider, as he has learned first hand that safety nets are critical. "If you have a skill or special training use that to your advantage. If you don't have a safety net or side business I think it's helpful to at least have an eye out for job opportunities and understand industry trends. I saw the warning signs in (my former) industry and it forced me to

---

© 2019 Dragonfly Ranch Consulting

create that backup plan."He shared that by being proactive, it spared him from the typical "lay off situations" where he would have been put out and just have to believe everything will be okay.

Now his side business has become a quickly growing full-time business and he and his wife could not be happier, nor prouder!

Max exclaims, "We are very excited to see what other great adventures await us. Now that I own a business I am continually thinking of ways to diversify."

You aren't quite done yet...keep going for a little more on Day 5!

© 2019 Dragonfly Ranch Consulting

LESSON: DAY 5

DAY 5 OUT OF THE BOX THINKING EXERCISES:

List 5 companies you could send a video resume to:

1. _____

2. _____

3. _____

4. _____

5. _____

List 3-5 people to start weekly Meeting of the Minds Networking Group with:

1. _____

2. _____

3. _____

4. _____

5. _____

Write out your 30 second personal commercial/"Elevator Speech":

© 2019 Dragonfly Ranch Consulting

GET CREATIVE! Now create a video of you delivering your 30 second personal commercial speech. What more would you need to do to polish that up and upload to YouTube?

Next, take a few minutes to look at Blogger or other Blogging sites. What would it take to upload your resume there and and add a brief bio, and maybe the video bio that your recorded? Add your notes on this here:

LIST 5 UPCOMING JOB FAIRS:

1. _____

2. _____

3. _____

4. _____

5. _____

Now add each of those to your calendar and your TO DO List. BE SURE TO ATTEND!

© 2019 Dragonfly Ranch Consulting

List YOUR own Out of the Box ideas here: (Remember, nothing is too crazy, as long as it is legal, right?) GO FOR IT, this is a safe zone for your thoughts and dreams!

© 2019 Dragonfly Ranch Consulting

© 2019 Dragonfly Ranch Consulting

So at this point, you are finished with the boot camp part of the guidebook. You've gotten organized, you've gathered the parts and pieces of the what you need to move toward finding your next job. But I just can't leaving you there, because I've got a few more tips for you to keep you going. So take a moment to read the last two chapters of the guidebook now.

"Ambition is the first step to success.
The second step is action."
~Author unknown

Chapter 9
NOW WHAT?

So it's been a week and you've dealt with a lot! Possibly all sorts of emotions, possibly lots of conversations with a multitude of people all about the same thing, wading through the fog and figuring out your next steps. But with all that and more, you've kept in motion. Instead of spending a week doing nothing but feeling sorry for yourself, you've been proactive, you've gotten yourself on track and you are now in the routine of your new job of Finding a New Job. You may be starting to apply for positions, and with that means you may be interviewing soon. You may be starting to meet with friends and connections to discuss job leads and opportunities. All of it can be very overwhelming and scary and exciting and all of the above, all at once! That's just part of this adventure. (The bright sides)!!!

Some days your routine will need to adjust a bit to accommodate meetings, etc. That's okay! Just be sure stick with the routine, even if it is an abbreviated day. Some people have asked me how to do that once they are going out on interviews, etc. They also want to know how to keep up with it when they've been forced to take a position that they only plan to keep for temporary. My advice is to simply do what works for you, but keep doing it!

© 2019 Dragonfly Ranch Consulting

ABBREVIATED DAY: GREAT THINGS COME IN SMALL
PACKAGES

For me, my abbreviated days looked something like:

30 MINUTE-EXERCISE

DAILY AGENDA—Review & Prioritize top 2 tasks for To Do List

30 MINUTE-EMAIL CHECK

2 HOURS-PRIORITY TASK TIME (Remember, worst for first)!

30 MINUTES-DAILY 3

1 HOUR-JOB SEARCHING

(If I could fit in more later in the day, great, if not, I was sure to write in ALL CAPS on my accomplishments for the day that I had an INTERVIEW or CONFERENCE/LUNCH MEETING w SO & SO). Those are time consuming, but necessary, and very big deals. So they are always worth an abbreviated day!

KEEPING YOUR OPTIONS OPEN

Trust me, I could write a whole other book on the impact of being slapped in the face for being a loyal employee when companies let go of great employees just short of retirement, (after people have put in decade(s) of butt-busting work for them). While it is VERY easy to be bitter, it is also important to keep in mind that if you have been blindsided, hopefully you have learned that being loyal to a company should never be your priority again. Businesses and organizations are not typically loyal to their employees. A friend of mine said it best when she shared a thought from her father. He told her that no employee is a permanent one. We are all really temporary in some way, shape or form from Day 1. Do NOT get me wrong. This is not an excuse to suddenly become a slacker, with lack of work ethic and develop a total disregard for having pride in a job well done. It simply means, if the grass is greener somewhere else, then maybe you need to graze in lusher pastures. Always look

© 2019 Dragonfly Ranch Consulting

out for YOU! Have your own back, because there are NO guarantees that any organization is going to watch it for you. Most are looking out for their bottom dollar and will can anyone's ass to save their own. Just saying. So from here on out, always keep your options open.

You can do this by keeping a "Maintenance Schedule" whether you have a job and you are looking for a career change, or if you simply took on a job somewhere to pay the bills. Simply, designate a minimum of 2-3 days/evenings per week, (maybe even while sitting in front of the tv, if it's not too distracting), to follow this ultra abbreviated schedule. It's extra condensed, because you need to keep up the hobby/interests at least 2-3 days per week, for life. (I mean, you know what they say, "All work and no play...," right?)

Please note, one thing that transitions is your Daily 3 now becomes your Weekly 3, BUT you need to actually talk to them. Put your Hands-free to use and call them while you are sitting in traffic, or while you walk the dog. But calendar and call. (One tip I like is to make sure all these people who you've recently reconnected with, stay connected, by putting them on your To DO List for their birthday, and every three months from there on out). Staying connected is how we continue to stay fresh on people's minds & visa versa! Seriously, we may need their help now, but they may need us later. (And it always feels good to help others by giving back and by paying it forward).

MAINTENANCE SCHEDULE: 2-3 Days Per Week

Review Agenda & Prioritize To Do List
30-60 MINUTES-TO DO LIST (Knock off 1 or 2 items—priorities first)!
30 MINUTES-WEEKLY 3 (a minimum of one person each day that you connect with)
30 MINUTES-JOB SEARCH
30 MINUTES-EMAIL CHECK

LESSON: Now what?

Well, when you've gotten this far, it is time to pat yourself on the back. Remember, you will only get as much out of this program as

© 2019 Dragonfly Ranch Consulting

your put in. It's time to reflect. If this is your first week with this program, then it was a hard one. If it is week 2 or more, then you probably have seen some customizations to the routine evolve. You've been customizing your To Do Lists, and over time there will be less and less of the Blindsided TO DOs, and more and more of your own that naturally come up as you work through your routine each day.

If ever you you feel yourself spiraling, start back on the program with a quick review of Day 1 and work through the schedule of Days 2, 3, 4 & 5, (and follow it diligently)! This will help you reset and get back on track with focus and productivity.

REFLECTION: I recommend taking time out at the end of each week to reflection on your progress. If you are finishing the first week of this program, <u>definitely</u> stop and reflect in the **NOTES:** section of your Daily Journal (or in this workbook). Write as much as you want--some weeks you may write just a little, other weeks you may find yourself pouring out tons of thoughts...there is no word count minimum or maximum, so just do it. (And I highly recommend continuing this practice once you find your new job. It will host a lot of great information for you as resource, while you always keep your options open)!

- What do I now understand more clearly about my "WHY?"
- How clearly do I understand my goal? Do I need to tweak it or is it good as it is?
- What were my biggest discoveries this week?
- What were my biggest "AH HA!" moments?
- What are my top 5 accomplishment this week I'm most proud of?
- What are my goals that I want to conquer next week?
- How am I different today, than I was the day before I started the Blindsided program?
- How can I help others get through a tough time like this?

WEEK 1 WRAP-UP (REFLECTION)

What do I now understand more clearly about my "WHY?"

© 2019 Dragonfly Ranch Consulting

How clearly do I understand my goal? Do I need to tweak it or is it good as it is?

What were my biggest discoveries this week?

What were my biggest "AH HA!" moments?

What are my top 5 accomplishments this week I'm most proud of?

What are my goals that I want to conquer next week?

How am I different today, than I was the day before I started the Blindsided program?

How can I help others get through a tough time like this?

© 2019 Dragonfly Ranch Consulting

WEEK 2 WRAP-UP (REFLECTION)

What do I now understand more clearly about my "WHY?"

How clearly do I understand my goal? Do I need to tweak it or is it good as it is?

What were my biggest discoveries this week?

What were my biggest "AH HA!" moments?

What are my top 5 accomplishments this week I'm most proud of?

What are my goals that I want to conquer next week?

How am I different today, than I was the day before I started the Blindsided program?

How can I help others get through a tough time like this?

© 2019 Dragonfly Ranch Consulting

WEEK 3 WRAP-UP (REFLECTION)

What do I now understand more clearly about my "WHY?"

How clearly do I understand my goal? Do I need to tweak it or is it good as it is?

What were my biggest discoveries this week?

What were my biggest "AH HA!" moments?

What are my top 5 accomplishments this week I'm most proud of?

What are my goals that I want to conquer next week?

How am I different today, than I was the day before I started the Blindsided program?

How can I help others get through a tough time like this?

© 2019 Dragonfly Ranch Consulting

WEEK 4 WRAP-UP (REFLECTION)

What do I now understand more clearly about my "WHY?"

How clearly do I understand my goal? Do I need to tweak it or is it good as it is?

What were my biggest discoveries this week?

What were my biggest "AH HA!" moments?

What are my top 5 accomplishments this week I'm most proud of?

What are my goals that I want to conquer next week?

How am I different today, than I was the day before I started the Blindsided program?

How can I help others get through a tough time like this?

© 2019 Dragonfly Ranch Consulting

"I find the best way to help someone is not to change them, but instead, help them to reveal the greatest version of themselves."
~Dr. Steve Maraboli

Chapter 10
YOUR LOVED ONES NEED SUPPORT TOO!

This chapter is a special note for the "Support System" of the person who has lost his/her job: (So show it to your support people. The sooner in the the process, the better.) Seriously, help them, to help you. Even better, encourage them to read the whole book! Please keep in mind, sometimes it is hard for your loved ones to 1) Wrap their minds around what is happening to you, and 2) You are changing your habits to be productive and successful, and sometimes that is also hard for some to understand.

I truly believe allowing them to read about the transformations you are going through so you may kick some booty on this job search process, will really help them see the whole picture.

What many people tend to forget is that when someone loses their job, oftentimes it brings on great stress to others as well. When my husband was laid off, we suddenly lost close to 66% of our income. OUCH! He had been our financial rock of the family. He had always encouraged me to do what I wanted with my career, because he could take care of us. Then that horrible day came when my rock was rocked. It was now up to me, solely, to keep us going. After almost 30 years of marriage, I was now the sole breadwinner for our family. (Secretly, I had always dreamed of making more money than my husband—but this was certainly NOT the way I wanted to do it)!

I mention this, because you may now be in the same position as the support to someone who has lost his/her job, and now need to be the sole provider, (while simultaneously needing to support that

© 2019 Dragonfly Ranch Consulting

loved one who is dazed and confused and trying to find his/her way toward new employment). But the reality is, there is some serious disbelief and despair YOU are probably going through, as well. I get it. It's awful to feel and it is awful to watch. Furthermore, there is no crystal ball to help you see that all will be okay, (and more importantly, when)!

Everyone is different on how they handle this. You can bury your head in the sand & pray this isn't happening, (but we both know that won't get you anywhere). OR! You could become super proactive.

- You can become the best cheerleader in the world and be the positive beacon in his/her life.

- You can become the ultimate pinnacle of resource for that person.

- You can become the networking guru of the universe and help make connections like crazy.

Whatever it is, when you find your way offering supporting, with the level of support that suits you both, you may also find yourself coping with this awful thing that has happened (to you too).

Here are a few tips for you on how to be a great support person:

1) Be sure you take care of yourself! Get doctor-approved exercise in everyday. You need to stay healthy through this process too! This is a stressful time, so give yourself permission to de-stress!
2) Read this book so you understand the process of the program that your loved one is trying to adapt to. It's hard, and the first week is the hardest. It will get easier, for both of you. Just trust that in order to move forward, your loved one needs to put all the moving pieces in place and stay in motion.
3) Become a positive Accountability Partner.

© 2019 Dragonfly Ranch Consulting

a) Do daily check-ins (at first—as weeks go by, every couple of days or so will suffice)
b) Ask about his/her top accomplishments of the day
c) Ask how the To Do List is going, and what are his/her next steps for the following day
d) Ask who his/her Daily 3 was for the day
e) Ask about the positive things he/she is discovering through this process

4) Help connect with YOUR resources. Ask people about leads, etc. then connect your loved one with those resources/people.
5) Share interesting articles, info., etc. in a kind, compassionate & respectful manner.
6) Establish times to connect and share each other's feelings. (Yes, that means YOU need to share your fears, concerns, etc. too)!
7) Be there.

You got this!

© 2019 Dragonfly Ranch Consulting

For additional success coaching services, contact us at:
www.TheDragonflyRanch.com

For specific coaching areas:
https://www.thedragonflyranch.com/business-coaching

For upcoming workshops, speaking events, and webinars:
https://www.thedragonflyranch.com/new-services

Author's Note:

I hope this book has been able to guide you through the bog of disbelief and helped you to either stay on track or get you back on track to looking for a new job. Be productive, be positive, & be persistent through this adventure. Life has a peculiar way of leading us to new discoveries, and this is one of the many in your life.

Wishing you well and encouraging you to keep at it, because when life shuts a door in your face, frickin' kick it down and find your own new window of opportunity!

YOU GOT THIS!

© 2019 Dragonfly Ranch Consulting

About the author

O. Michele Giacomini is a writer, educator, and a promoter of others. With over 14 years of business experience, PLUS, over 19 years working in the education industry & professional development, she has much to contribute to help bolster the success of others. When she isn't writing for a variety of publications, as well as her humorous Miss OMG books, you can find her coaching others for success in careers, business, writing/publishing and organizational strategies—or tending to her chickens on the country property she shares with her husband, in Northern California.

You can follow her on Facebook at:
https://www.facebook.com/TheDragonflyRanch/

and/or:
https://www.facebook.com/groups/springboardtosuccess/

Or follow her on LinkedIn:
O. Michele Giacomini

Other books by O. Michele Giacomini:

Looking for B.O.B. (BrightSides of Bull$#!+): Every Day

https://www.amazon.com/dp/153085721X

Surviving the Holidays: HELL-i-DAZE

https://www.amazon.com/dp/0578438399

© 2019 Dragonfly Ranch Consulting

www.ingramcontent.com/pod-product-compliance
Lightning Source LLC
Chambersburg PA
CBHW062049090426

42740CB00016B/3071